MONSOON RAINS & ICICLE DROPS

MONSOON
RAINS
& ICICLE
DROPS

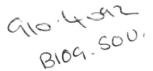
LIBBY SOUTHWELL WITH JOSEPHINE BROUARD

PIER
9

for Juz

CONTENTS

CHAPTER ONE

AS FAR AWAY FROM HOME AS YOU CAN BE

Well hello, I thought, here I am again, bug-eyed and wide awake in the middle of the night, this time somewhere in Outer Mongolia, trying not to think about things that make me sad. As I huddled in my down-lined, yak-skin sleeping bag on the floor of the *ger*—the nomadic equivalent of 'home'—I wondered if, after yet another totally unappetising meal of boiled mutton, I would ever be able to fall asleep. Shivering in my thermal underwear, wearing three pairs of woollen socks, two pairs of leggings, three thick jumpers, a scarf, woolly hat and gloves, I was obsessing about a dinner plate piled high with succulent pink lamb, crispy roasted rosemary potatoes and lashings of mint sauce.

Never mind that my real dinner was repeating on me and I was busting to relieve myself. The thought of leaving my tent in the freezing cold was bad enough, but the idea of squatting outdoors with wolves prowling about was enough to turn my stomach to steel.

Not a peep was coming from my friend Melon's sleeping bag and I felt a twinge of envy. How did she manage to sleep with a draft whistling around us, slipping beneath the felt walls of the *ger* and enveloping us in its icy fingers? Temperatures during the day here were bad enough, about 0°C to −10°C, but at night they dropped to −30°C. My bones felt so tense from the cold I sometimes thought they might shatter.

Sleep without vodka was proving elusive. Not so the night before in the free-flowing town of Olgii, where we'd been amazed to wake, still groggy, to discover that we had survived one of the biggest earthquakes to hit the USSR in decades. In that snowy town on the Kazakhstan border we had been only 100 kilometres from the quake's epicentre, but the first Melon and I registered of the calamity was when someone banged on our hotel room door in the early hours. Rising to investigate, thinking it was our driver waking us prematurely, we were almost trampled by huge Russian men in large Y-fronts, passports in hand, running in panic. What next? I thought, as I lay in the *ger*, safe if not snug, blowing little puffs of white cloud to amuse myself.

In the tent with us, on beds perched high on wooden frames, various members of our Kazakh host family snuffled, snored or wheezed gently as they slept. As I dozed, I heard almost imperceptible shuffles and raised my head to peer into the semi-darkness. In a corner of the *ger*, the grandfather of the family was rocking on his knees and chanting softly. Of course! It was time—the early hour notwithstanding—to pay homage to Allah in Mecca. I resigned myself to staying awake as I listened to the whispered prayers.

Only ten days before, Melon and I had criss-crossed the Gobi desert by jeep with our new nomad friends, Erdenbillag and Pooroosarung, occasionally stopping the vehicle to ride our horses, to hunt deer, milk camels or decamp a *ger* from a summer to a winter site. With the nomadic couple boasting a vocabulary of precisely five English words—Libby, Melon, Camel, Horse and

as far away from home as you can be

Good!—and Melon and I speaking virtually no Mongolian, communication was higgledy-piggledy and usually comical.

The Gobi had been relentlessly flat and treeless, with almost nothing to see except the camels, sheep, goats and horses we were herding along to the next stop. Early each evening we would huddle around the potbelly stove in search of warmth, piling the fire incessantly with yak dung before slinking off to bed, feral and sweaty in layers of clothing we never shed except to attend to a call of nature.

Occasionally, we would burst out laughing when we found ourselves reaching with relish for another draught of fermented mare's milk (*airag*) around the *ger* stove at night. But we hadn't yet been tempted to completely ditch our stash of Snickers bars or condensed milk for the local food. Deeply impressed by these Western confections that we shared with them, our Mongolian friends suggested we include some in our 'dowry' package when they tried to marry us off to two of their compatriots. In retrospect, Melon and I had been lucky to escape the Gobi as unmarried women.

I had been in Mongolia for almost two months now and Melon for about a month, but we were already behaving like locals. That is, smelling like the horses and sheep! Like me, Melon wasn't the sort to say no to any adventure or challenge. In fact, she'd seek out any chance to sing, dance, laugh or have fun—she'd even joined in a hair-raising gallop across the desert despite her lack of riding experience. Here though, the sheer cold was testing us both. Even during the day the sun seemed to want to slink off somewhere warmer.

Who needed sleep anyway? I thought, inching my way closer to the potbelly stove and the little warmth it gave off. I'd been running away from my life long enough. By now, there were two years of memories sandwiched between me and that awful day in December 2001 when the telephone in my Melbourne office rang and a New Zealand policeman asked, 'Is that Miss Elizabeth Southwell?'. I still cringed at the memory, despite the passage of time. But I didn't want to dwell on that sorrow now—if I had to lay awake then I'd rather remember the good times.

Lying in the *ger*, listening to Melon and our hosts breathing around me, I recalled vividly one of the happiest moments of my life—the first time that Justin told me he loved me. After years as close buddies, he'd taken my face in his hands, planted a passionate kiss on my lips and looked me in the eyes. 'Libby,' he had said, his nose millimetres from mine, 'I love, love, love, love you.' It was almost as if he was daring me to disagree with him.

It was 4 o'clock in the morning in my cottage in Melbourne when he had first made this declaration. Justin had flown down from Sydney for a party I was hosting and my girlfriends had swooned collectively when they finally met the colleague about whom I had talked for so long. Until that moment our five-year friendship had been platonic, but on that night everything changed. Eyes ablaze, he pulled me towards him and kissed me. 'Libby, I can't hide it anymore. I love you and I want to be with you.'

I was flabbergasted. 'What do you mean?' I'd squeaked, rubbing my bruised lips in disbelief. 'You're my friend Juz, what are you talking about?'

Without waiting for an answer I'd turned tail and run into my bedroom, unsure of how I was feeling and the implications that this kind of declaration might have on our friendship. It had taken me a while to come round to the idea, but when I got over the shock I realised I felt just as passionately about Justin as he did about me.

Once we had finally admitted our love for one another we'd called each other '*Mon Amour*' all the time. It was deliciously sensual and amorous and exciting ... just like our love affair. And it was also *très* French, which is how Justin and I both liked it. We loved *toute la belle* France and it seemed apt, having met the person with whom each of us wanted to spend the rest of our lives, that we should whisper endearments in the language of Françoise Hardy and Edith Piaf.

All through my travels across Asia, from the jungles of Nepal to the pine forests of Siberian Mongolia, with all the amazing things I had seen and done, the refrain was always the same. I still longed to share everything with him. Whenever I felt lonely and sad, or desperate and stressed, I also felt I could turn to Justin—he was a constant presence during my waking moments.

'*Mon Amour*, the world has changed for me and I can't go back,' he had written to me in one email. 'Pure love is my new world … a world where I can give all of myself and still be who I am. It is beyond what I dreamed was possible for me. I didn't believe it was possible to have this and still be me.' Now all that was gone.

As the early dawn light crept in through the *ger* flaps, I sighed with longing and let the memory of his impassioned words wash over me. I'd never known such love, never felt such joyful yearning for another person. When I was with Justin, I was happy, safe, and warm. Now, as much as I tried to hold that feeling close, *Mon Amour* had never seemed so far away.

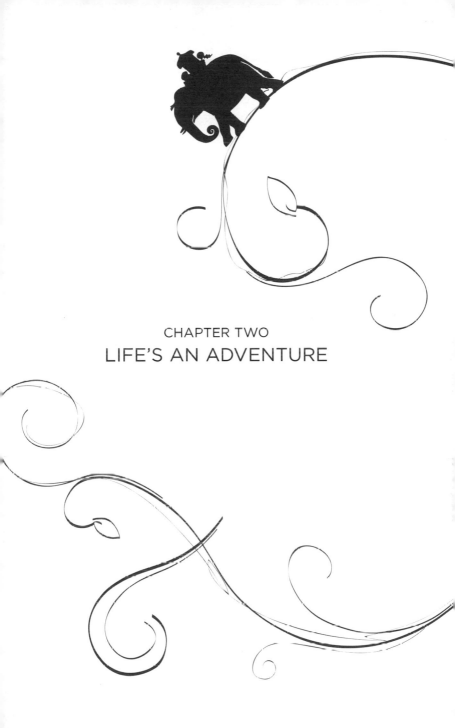

CHAPTER TWO
LIFE'S AN ADVENTURE

When I was a child all I cared about was running around our family farm in Camden on the southwest outskirts of Sydney, shrieking with excitement as my siblings and I played with our three cousins who lived next door.

In summer, we would swim all day in the dam between our two properties and swing from the trees like monkeys on tractor tyres suspended on branches overhanging the water.

It was an idyllic life filled with dogs, cats, birds, cattle, pigs, chooks and horses. My older brother, Hugh (always Hughdle to me), went to pony club on his horse, Apples, and I had a horse too, Peggy.

As a child I would dream of galloping, wind in my hair, over vast plains on a gleaming mare, but I found the reality in waking daylight a tad less romantic. So when Peggy died, I took to hooning around on tractors or climbing trees to scout the best place to build a cubby house.

My brother would often dare my older sister Annie and I to race each other on our mini-bikes as fast as we could to avoid the plovers that liked to dive and attack us. 'Let's go, c'mon, let's go,' he'd urge, and while Annie hung back I would take the bait. Having already been pecked on the skull by a magpie, my sister was usually less enthusiastic than her baby sister and if I was stupid enough to do it, well … she could always look forward to a laugh. She loved it when I would take to Hughdle's horse after yet another dare and inevitably get bucked off. There I was, peeing in my underpants with fright as

Apples gave me the heave-ho, but my sister's delight was enough to get me up and on again in no time.

Mum and Dad had two enormous chicken sheds on the Camden property with thousands of chooks that they sold to the big suppliers of frozen poultry, Ingham's and Steggles. Wild, curly-haired Neddy was our chicken keeper, a tough old bugger who mesmerised me with his long fingernails that he would use as screwdrivers when mending fences. During one electrical storm, lightning struck as Neddy crouched alongside one of the chicken sheds. After the storm, we noticed that Neddy's wrinkles had disappeared, replaced by skin that had been polished smooth and darkened a couple of shades. We gazed at Neddy, awestruck at Mother Nature's remarkable makeover.

Occasionally, personal catastrophes would threaten our Camden idyll. When our grandmother died unexpectedly during a hospital visit for a broken hip, my father was devastated. For the first time, I got a hint of the sensitive soul behind his exterior bluff.

Some years later, when a terrible drought affected the family business, the stress again took its toll on my father's nerves and he was forced to take time off work. For almost a year, while my uncle tended to office affairs, Mum took care of Dad until he got better. My parents have always been devoted to one another; it's hard to say exactly who looks after whom. Dad still says constantly to my mother, 'Oh Meg, would you slow down. I worry about you, Mum'.

In his younger years especially, Dad loved travelling and was passionate about anything Italian, even starting an Alfa–Lancia car dealership in our rural community as an adjunct to his agricultural machinery business. Dad's business had a lot of Italian customers, including local market gardeners in the district whom he would visit, anticipating another espresso or delicious lunch that was always offered. Many a Sunday afternoon he would spend listening to Italian tapes and mastering new Italian phrases.

I guess I was more like Dad than I realised, at least in terms of fascination with other cultures. I became besotted with the French language and culture after my father returned from sailing the Sydney to Noumea yacht race and brought home the boat's skipper and family, all of whom were—to my young impressionable mind—thoroughly enigmatic in their French ways. In those few weeks that Gilbert's family stayed with us, I became hooked. I took up French lessons in and out of school and much to my mother's amazement started cooking *à la française*.

Later, during my gangly pre-pubescence, Mum and Dad sent me to New Caledonia to live with Gilbert and his family for three months. This was in the mid-1980s during an intense political time for the French colony— the native Melanesians, or Kanaks as they are known, were seriously agitating for self-government; several Kanak leaders had recently been assassinated and civil war was threatening. This didn't deter my parents from dispatching their youngest—Gilbert reportedly had his yacht all set to sail to Brisbane if things got too risky.

From the moment I landed on Grande Terre, as the main island is known, conversation centred almost entirely on the nation's political developments, all of it in voluble and opinionated French. I would sit around the dining room table, everyone talking nineteen to the dozen in a language I could barely understand, and feel acutely my exclusion. But I learned to speak French, and to understand the regional politics—fast.

At boarding school, my teachers wanted to know why I couldn't be more like my sister Annie. Compared to her, I was a little feral devil; singing, burping, farting and giving cheek in general. One of my childhood friends and surrogate big sister, Prue, was a few years ahead of me at school and became what the boarding house mistress called 'a bad influence'.

We'd scull wine from casks we'd find lying around; smoke cigarettes in the gym storeroom; play 'truth, dare or double dare'; and challenge girls to ride up and down the dorm on our bunkhouse bed trundles. The boarding school mistress would walk into a dorm room full of girls playing cricket or volleyball and ask, 'What's this noise about?' She would barely break stride before identifying Prue and me as the instigators and packing us off to the headmaster. Prue and I didn't care. We found it a challenge to see how much we could annoy our keepers; in an environment we found mightily repressive, it was a way to keep ourselves entertained.

Boarders also loved the country parties that were an institution at most of Sydney's private schools. We would typically organise a huge celebration at the end of the year where we'd all get completely drunk, snog ten boys, vomit, go home, sleep, get up and move on to the next party. I would occasionally find myself at these parties with a boy's hand down my pants and sober up instantly, running away in fright.

As we grew older, we moved on to the infamous bachelor and spinster balls. One of my closest school friends, Kath Deal, fell madly in love with a country boy, Dave Englert, at one of these events, driving off into a dusty sunrise with him after an all-night hoedown. Hours later, Kath's distraught parents were anxiously searching for their fun-loving daughter.

She was eventually found, dishevelled and hung over, in the middle of the Hay plains in rural New South Wales, with her new boyfriend and a run-down ute. Stubbornly declaring, 'He's the one, I've got to have him,' Kath persisted and four years later, after playing him off against various other suitors, marched young Dave down the aisle.

As for me, marriage wasn't on my mind, but travel and a career were. Going to university was a given—in this respect, I wasn't at all interested in challenging the status quo. But first I had to decide where to study, and what. I finally decided on a commerce degree, majoring in agriculture and marketing, and headed to Orange in central western New South Wales.

When I finished university, my friend Jen and I landed a three-month contract assisting an agronomist in the cotton fields of Trangie, near Dubbo. We would drive roughly 500 kilometres a day in 40°C heat, hopping in and out of fields that were filled with goannas, snakes and wild pigs, checking for insects and bugs or any signs of crop infestation. Armed with heavy radioactive canisters for soil testing and rusty pipes that we used to scare off pigs and snakes, Jen and I would amuse ourselves as best we could during the long working days under the scorching sun. We would come home at dusk each day to a disgusting flat that looked like a concrete toilet block. It faced west and had no insulation so we'd get home, exhausted, only to lie down on our beds and fry.

In the night we'd go to the pub where the two of us would laugh over 'fire trucks'—vodka and red cordial mix—and relive the day's dramas. We'd try not to dwell on the fact that our neighbour back at the toilet block had recently been thrown into (and more recently released from) prison for dousing a relative with petrol, and then striking a match. We were, we clearly understood, a very long way from the sophisticated Big Smoke.

Working in a field one day during this time, we spotted a handsome young farmer driving past in a four-wheel drive and decided he was rather snooty when he didn't give us more than a passing glance. Considering we were usually covered head-to-toe in mud and swaddled in pipes and equipment, it would have been a miracle if he had identified us as female, but we were still mildly miffed by his inattention.

Later at the pub, however, we were introduced to the young farmer and swiftly discovered the handsome stranger wasn't such a snob after all. In fact, Jen was so impressed by him that she soon after broke up with a long-suffering beau and married the cotton farmer, Simon, instead.

Meanwhile, I applied for a 'proper' job as national marketing assistant for a rural merchandise, wool marketing, livestock and agricultural real estate company based in Sydney. The job interview was nerve-racking. Even though I had gone to school in the city, I'd become a right royal country bumpkin after three years' absence and barely knew my way around. Then, bang on my 21st birthday, the company called and offered me the position. I was overjoyed, happy to use my brain again and ready to take the city by storm.

Two busy years passed, filled with non-stop work and hard-core play, before I decided to do what every full-blooded Australian girl must: travel. In February 1995, I departed, with another school friend Cath Burgess, for London. Once we arrived a friend put us in touch with a doctor who regularly employed Australian girls to work in his Alpine chalet during the ski season. It was an exciting prospect—I loved skiing and wanted to go somewhere I could practise my French, so where better than the French Alps?

During the interview, the Sloane Square practitioner and his wife enquired as to our cooking prowess. Stumped for about a millisecond, Cath and I assured them we had the credentials and, with six months to spare before the season commenced, swiftly enrolled at the prestigious Leith's School of Food and Wine, so that we could soon acquire 'official' culinary skills.

In fact, Cath and I found we didn't learn a huge amount about cooking at Leith's that we didn't already know, but we met a lot of 'Jemimas' and 'Camillas' rounding out their finishing school experience and we learned a lot about the British obsession with 'puds'. Ultimately, the course was worth the tidy sum it cost us because it gave us entry to the kind of work that we sought. And, truth be told, I still enjoy turning out one of Leith's cold lemon soufflés from time to time.

In search of some sun while we awaited the start of the ski season and our chalet cooking jobs, Cath and I decided to visit the Greek island of Cos. Lying on the beach during our first week, we saw a magnificent yacht moored on the horizon and immediately started daydreaming about sailing to Turkey on this sleek piece of heaven. We even imagined we saw an Australian flag at the boat's stern and finally, after three days of endless fantasising, negotiated a speedboat lift halfway and swam the rest of the way to see the yacht up-close for ourselves. It was moored a fair way out and Cath wasn't a great swimmer, but I egged her on.

By the time we arrived, we could see the yacht was flying the Bermudan flag, not the Australian one, but Cath was half-drowning, so I decided it was no time to be shy.

'Excuse me, could you tell us what your flag is?' I managed to call out, between huge gulps of seawater, to a group of people at the yacht's stern. It was a very silly pretext for getting a conversation started, but I had three goals that day. The first was to climb aboard the yacht and land an invitation to sip a cocktail; the second was to be invited to stay for dinner and go for a bit of a sail; and the third was to get a job aboard for the summer and sail to Turkey.

Miraculously, Cath and I were indeed pulled aboard the rich man's plaything and offered a drink; we soon discovered the yacht was one of the finest 92-foot Royal Huisman specimens in the world, and belonged to a

German financier. We had barely caught our breath, however, when the Poms aboard ordered us to jump off again. They'd spotted the owner's nephew motoring toward us, so we were jettisoned like unwanted sea bass and could now look forward to swimming many kilometres back in very choppy waters! Poor Cath backstroked the entire way, barely able to lift her body out of the water when she reached shore 50 exhausting minutes later. I felt a bit guilty and grim, given that the excursion had been mainly my idea.

Two nights later, strolling around the village streets with another friend, Michelle, we bumped unexpectedly into four of the ship's crew. Cath and I found it hard not to be standoffish—we felt we'd been treated rather brusquely, but Charlie the skipper insisted on joining us for dinner. Hours later, we were all drinking like fish (or should that be, like lish?) and getting along famously.

Next thing, Charlie happened to ask about our sailing and cooking experience and, after we filled him in, offered Cath and me a job sailing on the *Cyclos II* and he was going to pay us US$50 dollars a day to do it! We were over-the-moon hysterical, hugging each other like lunatics, and decided to go dancing to celebrate. It didn't take us long to work out that the crew had their eyes on us, but there was no way I was going to snog anyone when I was going to be working with this mob for the next couple of months.

When one of the crew then went off with Michelle, Cath started to get cold feet. 'Maybe these guys are just a bunch of sleazes.' Cath argued. 'Who knows what they are capable of Libby. We don't know them from a bar of soap.'

I couldn't believe my ears. 'This is an opportunity of a lifetime, Cath, this is what we dreamed about!'

I was so forceful that, finally, at 5 o'clock in the morning, Cath caved in. 'Okay Lib, okay. All right, we'll go!'

And so, for the next few weeks we sailed, cooked, laughed and drank our way around the Mediterranean. Charlie later admitted that he wanted to sack us after the first night when Cath and I got tipsy and left a chook roasting in the oven for hours, before serving up a disastrous dinner. Luckily, our fare improved and they liked us enough to keep us on, although it might have been as much for entertainment as for culinary expertise. We parted in Turkey and promised to keep in touch.

Weeks later, back in London and weary of pouring wine at society weddings and charity balls peopled by the likes of Tim Jeffries, Hugh Grant and a gazillion Sloane Ranger nymphets, we called Charlie, desperate to escape. Sure enough, he was sailing the Mediterranean the following week and invited us back on board. We hopped on a plane to Mallorca and within days I had fallen head over heels in love.

Charlie was macho, sexy and fiery and certainly did not look 23 years older than me, though he was. He often treated me as if I was a bloody idiot and we consequently had enormous rows, but I stayed with him for months. Above all, we had such fun! I would put on a Tina Turner album and sing and dance while vacuuming, always entertaining myself as best I could, and Charlie would find me, laugh, and join in. We'd boogie madly before collapsing in a happy heap, domestic chores forsaken.

After some months of this, Charlie announced he was off to skipper a yacht in the Caribbean and my heart sank. 'Of course we'll see each other again,' he would reassure me, but could not be drawn on definite dates. I became miserable and bereft. Fortunately, November was drawing near and the Meribel ski season loomed. I took off to nurse my bruised heart in the Alps.

With my days filled with cooking meals and skiing, I was slowly recovering when one day the telephone rang and I happened to pick it up. It was Charlie. He told me to look outside the window and, sure enough, there he was, having flown in for two weeks to be with me. We had a blissful reunion, but when he left we both knew it was over.

Returning to Australia in November 1997, I soon landed a job as account executive with a boutique advertising agency that specialised in pharmaceutical and agricultural marketing. I rapidly settled in, enjoying the challenges and the camaraderie. Then, playing social tennis one evening after work, I met Patrick Corbally Stourton, or Paddy as he was called, an Englishman and art dealer who was over-the-top, loud, gregarious, hilarious, crazy, eccentric and passionate about Aboriginal art. I fell madly in love. Again.

Like Charlie, Paddy was enormous fun and blindingly, illuminatingly positive about everything in life. When I'd cook him a couscous with currants, pine nuts, capsicums and herbs, he would enthuse with complete sincerity, 'This is absolutely delicious! Ab-su-lu-te-ly delicious! Lobby, (as Paddy liked to call me) I could eat this every day! I really want to learn to cook … surely I can learn? Could you teach me to make something as totally delicious as this?'

The end result was I would do anything I could to please Paddy. So when he asked me to cook duck with Morello cherries for a 'who's who' dinner he was hosting, I was happy to oblige. After much preparation, I put the ducks in the oven on low heat. Meanwhile, unbeknown to me, Paddy started worrying about how much time was passing and decided to increase the oven temperature. Instead of my usual delicious slow-cooked dish, we ended up with tasteless, cindered morsels. I was ropable. Paddy thought it was hilarious and to make things worse, insisted on serving the guests the charred poultry slathered in cherry sauce, all the while telling everyone what a brilliant cook I was. Of course, not a single guest could finish the meal and people continued to talk about the fiasco months later.

Even at his most aggravating, Paddy was great company. He was the oldest 'naughty schoolboy' I had ever met and managed to make everyone around him laugh, whatever mischief he got up to. Even his fellow prisoners in a Malawi jail on Africa's east coast, where Paddy was incarcerated for two weeks for failing to wear a helmet while driving his motorbike, found his charm irresistible. While everyone feared he would be brutally assaulted during his stay, Paddy emerged as chipper as ever, having spent most of his time catching up on his reading. So charismatic was he that it took me a long while to recover from our short-lived romance when it became clear that Paddy did not reciprocate my devotion. He remained a wonderful friend, however.

One Friday, when I was still feeling bruised after being left by Paddy, my boss announced at after-work drinks that he'd hired a new account director. The new bloke, he said, was joining our office after a ski season in Chamonix in the French Alps. My ears pricked up. Skiing in Chamonix? That sounded like someone of like mind.

When we were introduced a few weeks later, I was too busy with an important business pitch to take much notice. Justin, the new 'suit', moved into an office next door to mine and we started talking, as colleagues do. We discovered we lived in the same suburb, both loved outdoor sports and had many friends in common. It wasn't long before we were making time to catch up in the morning over bowls of cereal at our desks, typically discussing our skiing, sailing, trekking and holiday adventures. He soon called me Lib, I called him Juz and we'd talk for hours about our travels. It was a wrench sometimes to pull ourselves away to do some work.

After a few months we decided to train together to compete in the Sydney City to Surf fun run. We'd meet most mornings in Sydney's eastern suburbs, and run for about an hour. Justin's wife occasionally popped into our offices to visit and seemed nice. She, Justin and I soon became social friends, often going out for dinner with others and spending group weekends away.

Justin was openly emotional. If he felt miserable, he would cry. His inner life seemed to be a roller coaster a great deal of the time: incredibly happy on occasions, in the depths of depression at other times. Just as he didn't seem to have any problem showing or expressing his feelings, he was comfortable if I did the same. I could always rant, be happy, excited and sad or even a little 'bitter and twisted' if I needed to vent; he was never thrown by any of it.

Life was full and I worked hard; in fact, lots of people labelled me a workaholic, although I liked to go full-bore after-hours too, surrounding myself with friends and running from one social engagement to another. It was nice, though, to have a kindred spirit at the office to talk camping, trekking and mountain climbing with—

someone who seemed to see and understand another side of me. I could tell Justin when I had fallen into bed with someone out of sheer loneliness and he would tell me about his feelings of insecurity at work. Deep down, he didn't want to continue his career in advertising; he spoke constantly of wanting to write a book, or start an outdoors business, even his own rock-climbing gym.

The closer we became, the more people would gossip, and it always mortified us. 'Lib, I'm really pissed off. Matt's asked me if I'm having an affair with you.' I would sigh inwardly, and shrug, having fielded the same questions myself. None of the insinuations were justified, but no matter how much we denied it, the muck seemed to stick. I would find myself in the bathroom occasionally at work drinks, close to tears, after someone again intimated that something sleazy was going on between Justin and me.

Eventually, about 18 months after Justin's arrival, I accepted a promotion and transfer to open a satellite office in Melbourne. I thought it would be a great opportunity to prove myself, and Justin seemed to feel the same way when I told him. It was only many months later that he told me that he went home that day and cried.

Living in separate cities, we emailed each other often and I was distressed to notice that Justin seemed to be falling apart. He had joined a new agency and occasionally visited Melbourne on business. When he did, I would lunch with a wrung-out, rake-thin emotional mess. His marriage hurt him. His job frustrated him. Unfulfilled, he seemed to be fading away in front of my eyes.

Then one day, lunching again in Melbourne, he announced he was leaving his wife. He seemed certain about his decision and sure enough, went through with it on his return to Sydney, reportedly telling his wife what she already knew—the relationship wasn't working.

As the divorce proceedings began, Justin and I continued to correspond. He started a string of affairs and shared the salacious details with me. He and his wife, he wrote, were both moving on. Sydney offered plenty of distractions, but as always with Justin, the mountains called. He resigned from his job and returned to Chamonix for another ski season. We continued to stay in touch by email.

I had my own worries to contend with, not least of all working with a colleague who would think nothing of ordering me around or belittling me in front of staff. Justin was one of the few friends who knew how often I would cry in the car park before collecting myself to face another day at work.

I was in Singapore opening an Asian satellite agency when I got news that tragedy had struck my circle. Again.

Four years earlier, I had mourned the deaths of two close friends who had died in a light plane crash when taking off from their rural property in Bungendore, near Canberra: twins Deuchar and Tamsin Davy. I first met Deuchar on holiday when I was about 14, but it was only later at university, when I shared digs with him for two years, that we grew very close. Deuchar and I lived in each other's pockets for those two years; we loved outdoor adventures and spent many weekends together hiking, flying or kayaking. We were such close friends that we would hang out together during the uni holidays and that was when I got to know his family, including Tamsin, his twin sister, and Nato, his older brother.

When I finished university and began work in the city, I'd still visit the Davy family farm at least once a month; it became like a second home to me. When Deuchar and Tamsin died, I grieved for months.

This time it was Dave, my friend Kath's husband—the same fellow who had swept her off in his ute after the bachelor and spinster ball. Driving his ute into the sun with his dog on the passenger seat early one morning, Dave didn't see an oncoming car and crashed, sending his car into a spin, killing himself, and his dog, almost instantly. I knew I had to fly home to be with Kath.

Seeing someone in so much pain is hard to watch. There was nothing I felt I could say or do to alleviate Kath's loss. Her world revolved around her husband and, not surprisingly, she was finding it impossible to contemplate a life without him. It was heartbreaking.

The experience crystallised a feeling I'd long had. It was a deep belief that we are all ultimately alone. I found myself thinking that I never wanted to be so in love that I could be devastated in the way Kath was now.

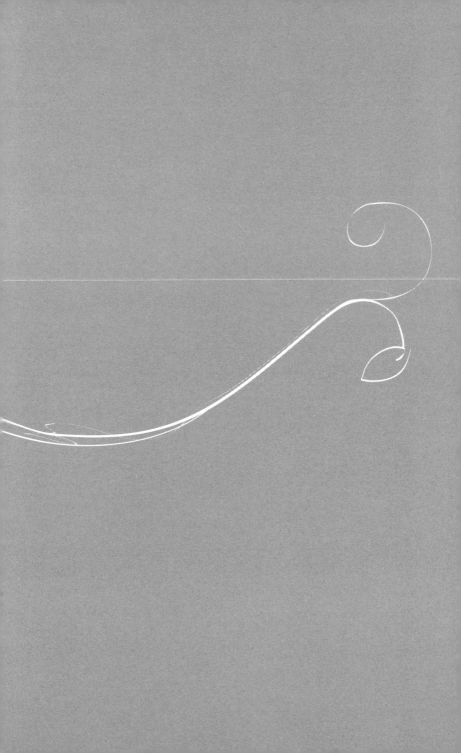

CHAPTER THREE
TRUE LOVE AT LAST

After a harrowing fortnight with Kath, I returned to the hectic pace of my Melbourne office. Between new business pitches, HR paperwork and the usual corporate grind of staff meetings and putting out client fires, I also started my own cooking school which I called Lobby Lobster, inspired by the nickname Paddy had given me on one of our beachside picnics when I suffered terrible sunburn.

Countless friends and acquaintances had professed to be in awe of my dinner party prowess and I was constantly bombarded for recipes, ideas and culinary advice. Eventually, flattered but exhausted by all the guidance sought by my friends, I invited them all to attend a weekly cooking class. Every Thursday at 6 pm we'd get together at my house and cook a three-course dinner for ten people—figs and gorgonzola wrapped in prosciutto for starters; barbecue quail in verjuice and grape bath for mains; chocolate and hazelnut torte for dessert—the lessons inevitably winding down after one too many wines.

Justin was still away in the French Alps, but I looked forward to the occasional emails he would send from Chamonix where, between ski thrills and spills, he was obviously doing some thinking.

From: Justin McDonald
To: Libby Southwell
Sent: 3.12 am Thursday 19 April 2001
Subject: See you soon

Libster,

How are you? I am looking forward to seeing you and talking face-to-face after four months away. Chamonix has its grip on me and with two weeks to go before I head back to Australia, I am already thinking about returning next year for the season. If I quit a job again to come here, I will totally destroy my prospects in advertising, but that's life. If no one will employ me, I guess I'll just have to employ myself.

Things here have been mixed. Skiing has been good, climbing terrible due to the weather, and a friend killed skiing here a week ago. Not good. My climbing tick-list has remained pretty much the same as it was four months ago, so yes, I'll have to come back. The skiing has been exhilarating, but the nightlife a little too much for these old bones. I'm looking forward to some rest in Sydney.

My history with women remains the same—unlucky and unsuccessful. I saw this beautiful girl out one night. Eyes were locked, worlds colliding, etc. She turned out to be Italian, a friend of friends. A meeting was arranged but thanks to food poisoning, she spent 24 hours vomiting up the entire contents of her stomach. Charming. Another meeting was arranged. We talked for hours, I thought 'Wow, what an incredible girl'. Then she returned to Italy and now I'll probably never see her again. I don't think she's in my stars.

So, two weeks to go and I head home to an Australian winter, divorce proceedings, the sale of the marital home, job and house hunting, and regurgitation of all my Chamonix stories to any friends willing to listen. It will be a reintegration into the real world (if that is possible) while dreaming of climbing ice couloirs, skiing unbelievable terrain and women with beautiful eyes. What's news with you?

Take care and I hope all is well. See you soon.
Justin

While in Chamonix Justin also corresponded with a close mutual friend of ours, David Sweeney, with whom both Justin and I had worked in Sydney. David and I still regularly kept in touch by phone and email, and he told me about a letter he'd received from Justin. At the time, both David and I were struck by Justin's typically pragmatic approach and how philosophical he sounded. Some months later, before heading off on another climbing adventure, Justin then gave me a copy he had kept of this same letter.

Dear David,

I went to a funeral this week of a guy I didn't know very well. His name was Julien and we all called him 'petit Julien'. He was 5'4" and French through and through. He died while skiing a very hard couloir off a mountain here.

The service was in French so I didn't understand all that was said. In fact, after five minutes I tuned out and thought about my own mortality.

Please take this seriously. If I die, I want you to organise a celebration service for me. I would like it to be in the park at Diamond Bay near Bondi.

I want you to say some words about who you knew me to be. I also want Angus, my brother, to say something, and then if anyone else wants to say something, they can. I don't want any religious shit. Not a thing. I forbid it.

I want some music: Pachelbel's *Canon* and something by Albinoni, I don't remember what it is called. Also, the Beethoven symphony, it is not called 'Joy to the World', but something like that. I also want Track 9 on the Verve album, *Urban Hymns*.

I know this is heavy, but what I am doing is inherently dangerous and I could get killed.

I wish I could tell my parents this, but it would scare them too much: I am happier than I have ever been and although I will do everything I can to avoid death, at least if I die it happened while I was doing what I loved.

I then want you to go out and have a huge night and do the things I like to do, dance, talk crap, have serious discussions and drink lots of Sambuca shots with six drops of Tabasco. When you dance, you must have a facial expression that communicates serious concentration (as I always do). No one is allowed to be serious. Chicks can cry during the service, but afterwards there can be no crying. My life has been fantastic and I want people to smile and laugh when I'm gone. Sorry to lay this on you, but I know you will do it for me.

Your friend always,
Justin

ps. We can talk about this when I get back.

By July 2001, with Justin returned to the advertising fold, our friendship resumed, though we were living in different cities—me still in Melbourne, him in Sydney. For the first time however, both of us were single and when I invited him to a party I was hosting, he seemed happy at the thought of a weekend away.

The night of the party arrived and my girlfriends, keen to meet the friend about whom they had heard so much, looked on appreciatively when Justin, fitter and more relaxed than I'd seen him for a long time, took to the dance floor. A few even admitted they thought him delicious and I laughed. Others swore Justin had eyes only for me, but I shrugged off those comments.

As the last of the party stragglers left and the worst of the mess was cleared up, a few of us made for bed. Justin was getting ready to sleep in the living room. I looked in on him to say goodnight and found him sitting on the lounge, looking thoughtful.

'Are you alright?' I said affectionately, feeling happy just to see him after all these months. He was such a good, dear friend! But Justin was looking at me strangely. 'Is something wrong?' I asked. And then suddenly he was up, taking me roughly in his arms, grabbing my shoulders, then my face. His eyes were piercing me in a way I found almost frightening.

'Libby, I love you. Love you. Love you. LOVE YOU.' Pause. 'Understand? This is not alcohol talking. This is me, Juz, your friend talking. I love you, Libs.'

I don't know what I said; I only remember my heart beating fast. Racing! I felt giddy and couldn't find anything to say. 'Juz, it's late, let's talk in the morning.' I turned and walked out, spending the next few hours in a daze.

When we were finally alone later the next night, after a succession of after-parties, Justin followed me into my cottage and I turned to him with trepidation. 'Some wine? Do you want to tell me all about France?' I offered by way of casual chitchat, but Justin was having none of it.

'Let's cut to the chase, Libby, I can't hide this anymore. I cannot lie one more day! I don't know what it means or what the consequences are; I just want it to be out in the open.' His feelings came out in a rush. He told me how all his recent girlfriends accused him of being in love with me, how his wife had been convinced his heart was in my hands, how even my friends at the party the night before, Melon especially, had told him how obvious it was. He said he'd wanted to tell me for ages; but he knew I would be frightened away.

'I can't hide it anymore, Libby,' he kept saying, over and over, until we parted for the night and I spent hours staring at the ceiling again. My heart was racing, my legs were wobbling; I felt as if someone had thrown a grenade into my arms. For years I had suppressed what I really felt for Justin; right then, I just couldn't take it in. I was scared of being hurt again; defensive; plain confused. The next day we drove to the airport, the pair of us pale-faced and tired from lack of sleep.

From: Libby Southwell
To: Justin McDonald
Sent: 4.53 pm Monday 23 July 2001
Subject: The morning after the party

Juzza,

It's official, I feel like a piece of pooh. Swollen glands, sore throat and really dragging my butt at work today whilst trying to be chipper—ooooh, it's a struggle. Too much partying, but what a lot of fun!

Thank you so much for making the effort to come down for the weekend. It was great to have you and the girls in town. It's a shame all of you don't live here ... we'd have a lot of fun.

It was also great to have a good chat at last and to catch up ... could have chatted all night long, however my eyes were falling out of my head. I really admire your openness and honesty, it's one of the things I most admire about you. And I'm pleased that you said what you said. I need some time to absorb what you've said now—you're right, it's a bit of a shock.

You've always been an amazing friend to me, Juz. The last thing I want is for either of us to rush into something, to hurt one another and jeopardise the amazing friendship we have. But ... without sounding pessimistic ... or even too optimistic ... I believe what you said on Saturday night ... will only strengthen our friendship.

Have had it with work today so I will say *adios amigo* and go home to an early night. Heaven!

Loov Lib xxx

From: Justin McDonald
To: Libby Southwell
Sent: 9.13 am Tuesday 24 July 24 2001
Subject: Re: The morning after the party

Lib,

I feel okay at this point, but I might hibernate for the next couple of weeks. The body has taken a pounding and needs rest.

I'm really glad I came down and met your friends. They are a great bunch and I'm sure I will see them again. The party was fantastic and I want to secure the cocktail blender spot at every party I go to in the future.

The weekend had its surprises. My 'cast off the lifeboats and bugger the consequences' attitude and the content of our early morning conversation really surprised me as much as it seemed to surprise you.

But at 5 am on Sunday morning I didn't care what the outcome, whether we would ever be friends again or not. Some things just need to be said and done. I regret nothing, though I'm not sure what it means. I would like it to be simple, but it's not. I hope as you say that one way or another, that our friendship gets stronger.

This will run its course and I'm willing to let it go wherever it wants to. Time will tell.

Take care,
Love Justin

Justin and I hadn't seen each other since my party but during this time, as we corresponded daily and called each other every night, our conversations became increasingly intimate. It was as if we were falling in love long-distance … strange, yet making perfect sense. We talked about a million things and began planning a skiing holiday together in Mt Hotham in the Victorian Snowy Mountains, with both of us flying in from our respective capital cities.

From: Justin McDonald
To: Libby Southwell
Sent: 1.50 pm Monday 6 August 2001
Subject: Lack of zzzzzzzzzzzzzz's all round

Good phone call. Lump in the chest and throat when I talked about some of my experiences and when I heard about yours. Teary-eyed at times. Glad we talked.

This lack of sleep is the same as when you start a normal relationship, except that we're doing it the other way round. Mental/emotional, then physical. I miss you, but I don't know why. You haven't been a constant in my life for such a long time, but now I want to talk to you and see you all the time. Sorry, we said we wouldn't do this by email.

Mt Hotham, Mt Hotham, the mantra continues. Bring on Mt Hotham, put me in a tent, fire up the coffee bomb, break out the sleeping bags, pour the red wine, stir the pot, stare up at the stars, see the condensation of our breath, the chill on our faces, the light from the fire ... can't wait.

Before our break alone together a 'first' that had me shivering at the thought—I flew to Queensland for a long-planned quick break with a friend, Georgie. Justin suggested he and I meet at Sydney airport where my plane was to stop en route to Melbourne. Excited at the thought I agreed.

As the time approached for my landing however, I found myself unbearably jittery. Justin and I were usually excited to see one another at any time—he was my close friend and fellow adventurer, after all—but now that we'd kissed and endlessly talked about our feelings, I was awash with emotions. Since his confession to me weeks earlier and our ensuing impassioned conversations, I was finding my defences steadily being eroded. It was difficult not to think about Justin every minute of the day.

The closer the plane got to Sydney, the faster my heart beat, until it felt like it was going to jump out of my chest. I had to do something, anything, other than just sit still, so within minutes, my friend Georgie had talked the stewards into allowing the two of us into the cockpit and had struck up a conversation with the pilot. It was good to talk about wind velocity and navigational hazards—anything other than replaying in my head, for the umpteenth time, the scenes of Justin and me.

But all too soon we landed and there he was in the arrivals hall as promised. After weeks of impassioned phone calls, long emails full of tacit declarations, we faced one another guardedly. I also looked at Justin properly, seemingly for the first time, and noticed how truly handsome he was. Georgie quickly headed off in search of a bookstore to give us time alone, but my connecting flight was called and my heart sank. We'd been together all of ten minutes. Then Justin spoke. 'You're not getting on that plane. I won't allow it. You're coming home with me.'

I was stunned. 'What do you mean? I've got work tomorrow, I've got no clean clothes.' I couldn't think straight. Was this really the same Justin with whom I'd once worked side-by-side, in whom I'd confided all my problems, with whom I'd trained and regularly got sozzled, sharing my heartaches and laughing delightedly at our private jokes?

The man I thought I knew seemed different today. He'd been so miserable for so long, now he seemed happy, newly minted. 'Let's cut to the chase Libby, I can't hide it any more. I can't lie any more. I love you, okay? I just can't suppress it any more. Everyone's always asking about us … well, they're right. I am in love with you and I can't hide it any more!'

Energised by his declarations, he set about getting my luggage off the plane while I sheepishly bade Georgie farewell. Still dazed, I allowed Justin to steer me to the car park. 'Mum's cooked three-day duck, we can go there for dinner. Hang on a minute.' Justin pulled out a mobile phone. 'Mum, is it okay if I bring a friend home for dinner?'

Meet Justin's parents now? It was all moving so fast. So far, that one kiss a month before when Justin had declared his love for me had been our only intimate romantic contact. We'd been very close friends for five years, but even after too many drinks, we'd always kept things platonic. Justin told me later that there were so many times he wanted to say and do more, but he'd always hesitated—he had been sure I would react badly. Suddenly, he loved me and there I was, having dinner with his parents and to my surprise, it was all going smoothly.

I met Ian and Jan who were warm, friendly and hospitable as I talked, listened and enjoyed the duck. But I felt preoccupied the entire time; it was a struggle to keep my reeling thoughts under control. Then the meal was over and Justin and I were alone at last. Driving home to his apartment, we fell silent, both of us deep in thought as we considered everything that had led to this moment.

There is something about male friends. No matter how close the friendship, the thought of being intimate with them physically, and of them seeing you naked, is a little bit frightening. It's a line that you just don't cross. And yet here I was, about to cross it.

Arriving at his apartment, we became as awkward as teenagers. But I didn't want to put up any further resistance; when Justin leaned forward to kiss me, I shut my eyes and hoped for the best. We kissed for hours and later, crawled into his bed and made love.

When we'd finished, we looked at each other and laughed. Such a relief! Everything felt more than good, it was skin-tinglingly perfect. This is so right, I remember thinking, I feel like I'm home. After all the initial confusion, I couldn't believe the depth of my feelings.

How long had I been forced to keep them under wraps, how long had I hidden the truth from myself! For the first time in my life, enveloped in Justin's loving embrace, I felt 100 per cent happy and safe.

From: Justin McDonald
To: Libby Southwell
Sent: 11.24 am Friday 7 September 2001
Subject: *Mon Amour*

My god ... In brief moments I imagined what you would look like under your jogging gear or the blue collar shirt and pearls, but I never thought that you would be the person with whom I would have the most passionate, sensual sex I've ever had.

Having breakfast in your office gave no indication of the connection we would have on so many levels. And there's so much more of our bodies and minds to explore.

Lib, this is much more exciting than being 16. Then it is just the newness of kissing someone, anyone, and the hormones at last being let out of the cage. It is no more than a physical reaction. This is so much more.

The friendship seems insignificant compared to how I feel about you now. The last four or five years was a warm-up for the real event, a prelude to something beautiful that will carry us into the future.

À vendredi ma belle
Juz

From: Justin McDonald
To: Libby Southwell
Sent: 5.57 pm Tuesday 18 September 2001
Subject: Red letter day

Divorce papers came through.

Speak to you tonight *mon petit lapin fou avec les cheveux bouclés* [my little rabbit with curly hair].

From: Justin McDonald
To: Libby Southwell
Sent: 8.44 am Monday 24 September 2001
Subject: *Re:* The weekend

What can I say?

What an amazing weekend. I haven't got the time right here and now to say how I feel about you, about spending time with you and about our conversations, except to say I have lived without you for so long and now I don't want to live apart from you in the future.

Thank you for such a fantastic weekend.

Love Juz

Justin and I never lived in the same city during those first heady months of our relationship, but that didn't stop us from seeing each other almost every weekend, speaking and corresponding daily and planning an entire life together, right down to how many children we would have.

From: Justin McDonald
To: Libby Southwell
Sent: 11.30 am Tuesday 25 September 2001
Subject: *Mon Amour*

Lib, I love you. I want to give you two things: solid
roots that are unchanging and will always be there,
and wings to do whatever you want.

From: Justin McDonald
To: Libby Southwell
Sent: 1.56 pm Thursday 11 October 2001
Subject: Dreams

I am keeping all these emails. This feels really weird
to write but I want our kids to read them. It
probably will bore them to tears, little buggers.

From: Libby Southwell
To: Justin McDonald
Sent: 5.00 pm Thursday 11 October 2001
Subject: Re: Dreams

Darling,

I can't wait for you to be the father of my children.
I know you will be amazing with the kids. What an
incredible time we have to look forward to.

So many adventures and challenges to be had. And
this is only the beginning.

Have fun at the climbing gym tonight. xxx

From: Justin McDonald
To: Libby Southwell
Sent: 2.53 pm Tuesday 16 October 2001
Subject: Missing you

Mon Amour, I want to come home tonight, have a bath with you, then a glass of wine with dinner, then crawl into bed and talk and cuddle. I want to run my hands along the violin, spoon you and put my face in your beautiful hair and breathe in your glorious aroma. I want to feel your cold bottom against my hips and listen to you talk about your day. I want to fall asleep listening to the sound of your breath as you sleep.

Have a good day, *ma cherie*.

Then Justin resigned from his advertising agency job—everyone knew full well that his heart was not in it—and made plans to visit New Zealand for six weeks and climb Mt Cook. Before leaving though, *Mon Amour* moved to Melbourne to live with me in my tiny Richmond terrace. On his return from New Zealand, he and I planned to marry and have children. We were excited at the prospect of living together for the rest of our lives, but in complete agreement that before settling in and looking for a job, Justin should climb a few mountains.

Mountain climbing was Justin's supreme passion; it was utterly pointless to stop him from doing what he loved. For too long, Justin had suppressed his life's desires; it was time now for him to realise some of his dreams.

From: Justin McDonald
To: Libby Southwell
Sent: 4.14 pm Friday 19 October 2001
Subject: Going Away

I am going to miss you so much when I go away. I will be thinking of you all the time. There is a lot of sitting around in mountaineering, that's another thing I love, the time you have to think. It's like before there was radio or television, there was nothing to do but think. When the weather is bad you pretty much spend all day inside a hut in your sleeping bag having cups of tea and eating. You can play with ideas and throw them around in your head. You stare out of the hut window at the howling wind and hear the snow hitting the glass with force.

I want to take you with me in winter so you can see the beautiful blanket of snow on the awesome landscape, like the Alps but without the lights in the valley below, jagged peaks overhead and the pink sunset over Mt Cook.

I want you to be with me always, not just in the mountains but even in the mundane things of domestic living. I love you so much; my heart is bursting with happiness.

From: Libby Southwell
To: Justin McDonald
Sent: 8.00 am Friday 16 November 2001
Subject: I love you

Mon Amour,

I hate goodbyes; I have never been good at them. My heart ached this morning when I said goodbye to you. It was as if something had been taken from it. I realised for the first time what it would be like to have you taken away from me. In such a short time my love for you and our love for each other has grown so deep and so strong. I am sure for other people it takes years and that in some cases they never experience it.

I was not sure what to say to you and was reluctant to say what I really thought. 'Please be careful, I will miss you terribly, please come back safely.'

I didn't want to say these things to you as I totally respect what you are doing and what you are about to embark on. I admire you so much. This is a dream come true for you and you deserve it. I want you to live every second of it with passion and happiness.

There may be times when I go off and do my own thing as well. I know you will respect my decision to do this solo. I cannot believe what a wonderful relationship I have with you—it blows my mind. Our phone conversation was beautiful and intimate. I love you my darling,

16 November 2001

Ma folle fée,

I am feeling both sad and excited. After the plane took off from Sydney it flew over Bundeena and the beach, where it seems like only yesterday we swam naked and had a running race along the sand. This adventure we have been living together is fantastic.

I feel sad because it feels like I am leaving a part of my soul in Richmond. But I take with me the thoughts, feelings and emotions I have for you. I love you so much. These words seem to grow in meaning every day.

Justin

From: Libby Southwell
Sent: 9.22 am Monday 19 November 2001
To: Justin McDonald
Subject: My Day

Good morning darling. It sounds cold where you are and a tad miserable. I am glad there is a potbelly stove for you to sit by and write, read and sleep. Well, weekend one down. I know that is a bad way to think, but I was thinking how we are both missing each other terribly. I think it will be easier for you once you get onto the mountains. Bring on December 21, I say...

20 November 2001

Ma folle fée,

I felt a little scared today as the bus drove to Mt Cook. It's the uncertainty of the outcome—testing myself and not knowing how I will come up. But I guess that is what I love about this, knowing that success is not assured, but is something that needs to be struggled for and won. My stomach churns a little because it is not a game. I can't wait to be in the mountains with you, to climb a mountain and stand on the top with you. In this hut in Mt Cook village I see myself in nine months with you doing what I am doing now on my own. Love you.

Juzza

From: Libby Southwell
To: Justin McDonald
Sent: 5:00 pm 21 November 2001
Subject: Re: Dreams

Mon Amour,

I am missing you so much. More than I ever imagined.

You are so precious to me. I have never loved anyone like this or experienced the love I receive from you from anyone else. I have never been so sure about things—about marrying you, about having children with you and about spending the

58

rest of my life with you. I have no questions, no doubt, nothing but completeness.

I look at your picture every day. I read your postcards every night when I go to bed. I read them over and over again. I hug my pillow all night long and I shut my eyes and picture you.

All I want for you is happiness. I want you to relish in this adventure you are embarking on. I want you to feel freedom and love and know that I will always be supporting you in every aspect of life.

Climb those mountains *Mon Amour* and sing from the depths of love when you reach the summit. I am here for you. I love you!

26 November 2001
Beautiful,

Never feel guilty about what you say to me, nor how we interact. I would never want you to not express how you feel, or feel that you have to think or feel something you don't.

Your feeling sad upsets me, but it doesn't affect what I am doing here. I am enjoying myself and fulfilling the dreams I want to fulfil. I miss you and think about you nearly every moment ('Put crampon in snow there; I love Lib', something like that). It's hard to explain, but it's as if I am carrying a part of you inside me. I think about what we have done, all the good times, about our bodies together.

I also think about the future, about the moment our children are born, the look on your face, me holding your hand tight as a little person who is half me, half you enters the world. I am tearing up as I write this.

I don't want us to only have happy conversations because this is not a TV sitcom. Our relationship is based upon honesty and openness; if either of us feels like shit then we should say so. Besides, it would never work if either of us pretended we were happy. We would see through each other straight away.

Mon Amour, just got back from climbing a mountain!!!!! Yea ha. Left the hut at about 5.30 am on the only beautiful day we have had so far. I walked alone up a snowy ridge for about four hours. The snow at the top was soft and I sank to my knees with each step. As I got higher the snow hardened and it was like walking in a park. I crossed two valleys, traversed a glacier, climbed to a saddle on a 50-degree snow slope, climbed around the mountain and then ascended a steep snow slope to a rocky step.

I climbed through the easy rock bank and got to the snowy summit. I sat on the summit for about 10 minutes and took in the glorious day, then headed down. By the time I got down, the snow was soft and I was pot-holing the entire way back. Got back to the hut at 2.30 pm. It was sensational. Something we can do together next year.

Mon Amour, I love you so much, you are the person with whom I am going to spend the rest of my life. That makes me feel so happy and I want you to be happy. I love you my beautiful fairy.

2 December 2001

Dear Fairy,

When I put down the phone last night, I went to the huge windows that overlook the mountains and valleys in the distance. I felt this longing to be near you, I felt jealous of the blokes you went to dinner with on Friday because they had the chance to see you and talk with you. My heart was actually aching, there was a lump in my throat and I wanted to cry.

I walked to my room for no particular reason, and then walked back to the windows. I repeated this twice. I was a little shocked by the power and strength of this feeling that gripped me. I am missing you so much I am in physical pain.

I eventually grabbed my mobile phone and walked into a field. I looked up towards the Tasman Valley where New Zealand's longest glacier is. The light was strange. It was hazy up the valley, as if someone had placed a strong filter in front of the scene, giving everything a strong blue cast. I looked at this magnificent view, alone, and felt such yearning for you. I wrote the SMS messages to you with that view in front of me.

What a magnificent pain. To care about someone so much that separation from them causes actual physical pain.

Soul mate! I hated that expression—overused and not possible, in my mind. We are alone in this world, how can one person be the only person for me? I was wrong. In you, I have found all the good things in that expression: my best buddy, my best friend, insatiable passion and deep, beautiful love. *Mon Amour*, I have given you my heart and it hurts when we are not together.

Je t'aime and *je t'adore*.
Justin xoxo

From: Libby Southwell
To: Justin McDonald
Sent: 8.26 pm Wednesday 5 December 2001
Subject: Dark thoughts

A world without Juz ... not something I want to ever imagine. When I think about a life without you I don't think of us going our separate ways, because this will not happen. No, I think of a life when you leave this world. It kills me ... and I instantly go to my time with Kath when Dave died.

My memories of those weeks are still so vivid, I feel sick. I see her now and how she is dealing with life, and I now understand more than ever how she must feel.

In March I had never experienced true love; however, now I have and am with you. So I do understand what it must feel like to lose your lifetime love, buddy and best friend.

I know it's not a particularly happy topic, however that's what I am thinking. Yuk yuk yuk. Thinking about a life without you is far too painful.

Darling I love you from the end of my little pinkie toe. It's so deep. It's a deepness that a lot of people would find scary, however for me, it is nothing but right.

The fairy. xxxxxooooooxxxxxxxx

From: Libby Southwell
To: Justin McDonald
Sent: 10.44 am Tuesday 11 December 2001
Subject: Feelings

Morning my gorgeous beautiful love ...

I cannot stop thinking about you. I love hearing people talk about you. Sometimes I pretend I'm not listening and eavesdrop and when they talk about you, I feel warm and fuzzy. I think to myself, they are talking about a man that I love with whom I will be for the rest of my life.

When they ask me how I feel about you, I explode with excitement and happiness and say, 'I love him so much'. When I hear Mum and my sister talk about you ... they ask about you in such an endearing way ... though they barely know you. They think the world of you because of who you are and also because of how happy you make me. That makes them happy.

My darling I am bursting with love and happiness. Not long to go before we can lie in each other's arms, cuddled up together, laughing, chatting, crying and dreaming—all the wonderful things!

So much more to talk about with you face to face when I see you next week.

Je t'aime, je t'adore
Fairy xxxxxx

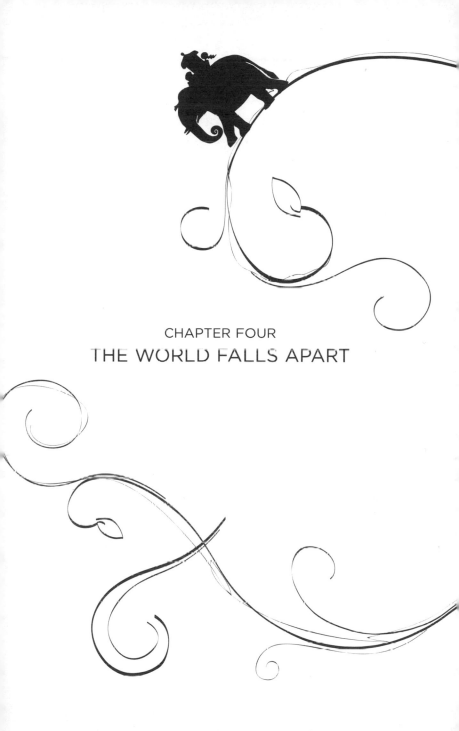

CHAPTER FOUR
THE WORLD FALLS APART

It was just before 4 pm on Friday 14 December 2001, and I was running out my office door to present a television commercial to a client when the telephone rang. I had so much going on that I almost ignored the call, but something made me pick it up.

I said, 'Hello', and a voice asked, 'Is this Miss Elizabeth Southwell?'

'Yes?'

'My name's Constable Sutherland. There's been an accident involving Justin McDonald. He's fallen down a crevasse on Mt Cook. Our rescue team hasn't reached him yet, but they're on their way. We don't know what the situation is, but we will keep you informed. This is my number …'

I said, very calmly, 'Okay, what do I do?' and I think the policeman repeated that he would call me again when he had more news. From there on, everything became surreal.

I think I paced up and down my office, then I remember walking into the office lift and going up and down about a dozen times. Finally, a colleague noticed that I was pacing and asked, 'What's happened, Libby?'

It was then I began to cry. I didn't have many facts to hand, but I felt already that Justin was not going to survive. Justin and I had talked a million times about mountaineering and falling down crevasses, we had even practised rescue techniques in the park, and now this had happened. My head felt like it would explode; my heart felt as cold as iron. Another work friend put her arm around me and, between sobs, I tried to tell her what happened. But I was barely in control.

I hadn't asked the constable any sensible questions and in my shock straight afterwards, I had mislaid the telephone numbers he'd given me. As colleagues and friends began to mill around, someone found my scribbles and, painstakingly, slowly, as if in a fog, I realised I had to do something—at least let key people know what was happening.

The first call, to Justin's parents, was the most awful one I have ever had to make in my life. Ian sounded happy and surprised to hear my voice. Then I told him what the constable had told me.

'What? Who? Where? Who is with him? What do you mean?' Even as I struggled to find the words, it was clear that Justin's father could not digest what he was hearing. Justin's mum, Jan, took the receiver and, gravely calm, listened to me repeat the horrible news.

Then Constable Sutherland called me back. He told me Justin had died. I was in my office surrounded by people, but I felt completely out of reach of any person, or any comfort. It was as if knives were ripping me apart; I began howling. I couldn't stop wailing at the top of my voice. People were crying around me, too. Everyone was in shock. Then the phone rang again with more news. It took me a while to figure out what they were trying to tell me … Justin was alive!

It was just too much to take in. I couldn't stop crying. At my core though, I felt numb. The telephone was ringing. And ringing. The world seemed completely out of control. I looked up and saw my friends, Pete, John and Georgie. What were they doing here, now? I discovered later that a former flatmate, Emma, had stopped in at my apartment earlier that day to use the toilet (she still had a key). The phone had rung while she was there and she had answered. It was Constable Sutherland in New Zealand trying to locate me. Emma had quickly guessed that something had gone horribly wrong, and had immediately started rounding up my close friends, which was why they were suddenly there.

Georgie led me out of the office and we drove to Pete and John's house nearby. En route, Georgie stopped off at her house to collect a gift she'd bought for me for Christmas: a framed photograph of Justin and me. At Pete and John's house the phone seemed to ring incessantly. Justin's parents called; his brother Alistair rang from the US; and his other brother, Angus, called from Byron Bay. Like Buddhist lamas, we chanted to one another, 'Justin will pull through, Justin will pull through'. I went and sat outside at one stage, in anguish, and stared at the framed photograph of *Mon Amour* and me and I pleaded with Justin. 'C'mon Justin … come on … don't leave me, please don't leave me.'

Then another call, and more bad news: they couldn't get Justin off the mountain; it was too windy. There were avalanches and these were making it too dangerous for the rescue team to land. There was concern that they might not be able to reach him.

I had to call my parents. By now I wanted to talk to those I loved most about what was unfolding. I had shared a lot with Mum in letters; she and Dad both knew that Justin and I planned to marry. She just kept saying in a soothing voice, 'Darling, darling, we love you, it will be alright,' as I cried into the receiver. What else could she say?

I could almost feel Mum looking at Dad, who I sensed was standing right next to her. 'Darling, we love you … call us as soon as you have more news.'

My friends were trying to get me to eat, everyone acting as if things were going to return to normal soon. All I could do was stare at the photo and close my eyes and whisper, 'Come on Juz, you can do it'.

Around 8 pm that night, four hours after the first call, Constable Sutherland rang and said Justin was off the mountain and being flown in a helicopter to a hospital in Christchurch.

When he arrived safely at Christchurch, a doctor rang and said, 'We've had to open his heart. He's in surgery now.' The doctor called again later, profoundly aware of the importance of his words. He spoke exceptionally slowly and calmly, 'He's out of surgery and on life support. Please know that we have done everything we possibly can.'

By this stage, various friends had arranged to get me on a 6 am flight from Melbourne to Sydney to meet Justin's parents and then fly on with them to New Zealand to be at Justin's bedside. But a part of me kept thinking, I will never see him again. I couldn't shake the feeling that he wasn't going to make it, while at the same time I was furious that I could think this way.

The love we shared had been too good to be true. I knew Justin was the happiest he'd ever been when he left me to go climbing in New Zealand; how could it end this way? Not now, when we'd come together at last.

Finally, in a dreadful fog of thoughts and emotions, I fell into an exhausted doze when the phone rang again. It was Jan, Justin's mum.

'Darling,' she said, 'he hasn't made it. Justin's had a cardiac arrest.'

It was 2 am in Melbourne when Justin's mother called me; about 4 am New Zealand time when Justin died. They say that people often let go then. They hold on for as long as they can, but if they need to let go, they do it just before dawn.

Transcript of Statement:
1230 hrs 15 December 2001
Mt Cook Visitors Centre

Andrew Ronald PEACOCK states:

That is my full name. I was born on the 16/04/67 (34 yrs).

I am speaking to Constable Greg SUTHERLAND about a climbing accident on the 14/12/01 at Mt Cook where my friend Justin Dawson McDonald was killed. I have known Justin for about five years and we are climbing companions and social friends.

Justin travelled to New Zealand about the 15th of November 2001 to climb in the Mt Cook area. I had planned to join him on the 6th of December 2001. I flew into Queenstown Airport and rented a car and drove to Mt Cook.

Justin and I flew into Plateau Hut on 7th December and stayed there for three nights. During this time, we climbed Silberhorn and managed to get four fifths of the way up before the weather closed in. We later flew out of Plateau Hut back to the village. We next planned to go up the Hooker and stay at Empress Hut.

On the 12th December Justin and I walked into Gardiner Hut from the Whitehorse Camp ground. We stayed one night at Gardiner and on the 13th we walked to Empress Hut. This took about 2.5 hours. After the radio check that night we decided to climb to the low peak of Mt Cook via the North West Couloir the next morning. At about 2.30 am on the 14th December we got up and left the Empress Hut at 3.15 am. We took all of our gear as we planned to stay at Gardiner Hut that night.

We walked to the best of the North West Couloir climb (marked 2.49 on the route guidebook). There we dumped our main packs and all the gear we did not require. This took 45 minutes. We started climbing at about 4.15 am. It was a straightforward climb to the summit of the Low Peak. We must have reached the summit at about 9 am.

We began to traverse the ridge to Porters Col, but felt unhappy with the ice conditions. We elected to down-climb 60 metres and traverse under the ridge towards Porters Col before reaching a place where we decided to abseil down to the snow slope below the bluffs.

The first two abseils were uneventful (about 60 metres each). For the 3rd abseil anchor, a nut [metal wedge] was placed in the rock. I placed this nut and backed it up with a number 1 size Camelot [spring-loaded camming device]. This was placed by me in a different rock crack and was loosely attached to the rope as a backup in the event the nut failed.

I fed the rope through a sling attached to the nut and abseiled 60 metres to the snow slope uneventfully. The protection held well, the nut did not dislodge and the backup was not needed.

Justin would have removed the Camelot and abseiled down to me using just the nut as an anchor. This nut was to be left in the rock.

Justin was coming down. He was abseiling 5–10 metres above me and it appeared he was swinging to the right before he fell towards me with the ropes and hit the snow slope 2 metres to my right and 3 metres below me. He then slid at high speed around 250 metres down the slope, the last part of which was out of my sight. Before I lost sight of him, the contour of the ground made him slide around the side of a large serac [ice cliff].

I down-climbed to the edge of an ice hole where I saw a large bloodstain. This took me 30 minutes. I saw the ends of our rope also coming out of this hole. The snow all around this area was very soft and I used a metal stake to make a poor anchor in the snow. I called out to Justin, but there was no response. I pulled his rope until it was tight and I could pull it no further. I gave three distinct tugs and got three distinct tugs back from Justin.

I imagined that if I continued to pull on the rope, I might be able to assist him climb out. But it was obvious that he was unable to climb, as the rope was not moving. I tied off the rope to the anchor, and then with a section of slack rope I crawled downwards along the snow bridge to a point where I could look into the slot. Justin was lying wedged in a narrow ice tube about 20 metres below me at that point, or 30 metres from the anchor. I yelled his name and got no response, but with repeated tries he moved his head and asked me to come down and help him. I asked him what injuries he had and he said 'none', but said he was very weak or tired.

I then knotted the ends of the ropes I had with me and managed to slide a loop of rope into the crevasse so that Justin could have grabbed the loop with his one free hand that I could see. I then crawled back to the anchor and pulled on the rope, but he couldn't hang on.

I then went back down to see him and told him I was going to get help from Search and Rescue as I couldn't abseil down safely to him. The crevasse was very narrow.

Again, he said that he wanted me to come down and help him, so I took off my helmet and tried to get into the slot to come down, but only ended up knocking down soft sections of the snow, which then fell on top of him. Now only his one free hand was visible. I yelled at him and he moved his hand in acknowledgment. (His hand was the only thing that was visible above the snow now).

A few minutes later after thinking about my options I yelled down again, but got no response. I crawled back to the anchor and left the area aiming to get back to Empress Hut and call Search and Rescue.

I began to down-climb through the crevasse field below us but it proved impossible so I climbed up again and traversed to my right to the rocky buttress and began a combination of down-climbing and traversing until I crossed our original ascent route up the gully. I down-climbed the gully to our packs and it then took me about 25 minutes to cross the lower Empress Shelf to the hut where I used the radio to call for help.

The accident occurred about 11.30 am to 12 noon. I would have left Justin at about 1.15 pm.

I recovered the nut from the rope lying on the snow when I first reached the edge of the crevasse that Justin had fallen into. It had obviously popped out of the rock as Justin was abseiling. I gave it to the police the following day.

We are both experienced mountaineers and rock climbers. Justin is a very good ice climber, but less experienced on moderate alpine terrain. I am a more experienced rock climber than Justin. We have both climbed in the Mt Cook National Park previously. I have climbed here on three separate trips as well as in Nepal, central Asia, Canada, USA and Europe. Justin has climbed mainly in Australia, New Zealand and France.

I have read this statement and it is true and correct.

I attended the inquest into Justin's death in New Zealand in early March 2002, with his mother, Jan. A few days after I returned, on 17 March (St Patrick's Day), I turned 30 and my friends arranged a party for me, trying to convince themselves—and me—that this might cheer me up. A celebration was the last thing I wanted, but I didn't have the energy to oppose any suggestions, especially those that were well-intentioned. I dreaded the party and lay weeping as the sun rose on the loneliest day of my life.

That night, wearing a woeful belly dancer costume and an attempted smile that was more of a grimace, I willed myself to make small talk with the 20-odd friends assembled. But I couldn't do it. I left early, returning to the solace of my house where I could cry without shame, surrounded by Justin's possessions.

I loved having his bicycle, pictures, clothes and sportswear around me. When I lay in bed, I'd imagine him there, lying with me, and almost believed I could smell him. I didn't want to kill myself, but I didn't want to be alive either. Not without Justin.

The weeks dragged by. Colleagues and friends would occasionally comment how gaunt I was, but somehow I got through the days. I would brush off the earnest, worried questioning, but in my heart of hearts, I couldn't see an end to my despair. In July I had a visit from Paddy, with whom I'd stayed friendly, and he bluntly told me he'd never seen anyone so miserable. He introduced me to his new girlfriend, Anya Rowlands, and we took to each other instantly.

She helped me prepare a small dinner party I was holding for her, Paddy and a few friends, and as we chopped vegetables together, she burst unexpectedly into tears.

'I can't bear to see you like this; I can't stand the fact that this happened to you. I've only been with Paddy for a few months and I feel like we've been together forever,' she explained between big gulps. 'We feel like old souls. I can't imagine how I would feel if I lost Paddy now …'

She was compassionate, and she understood. Justin and I had also felt like 'old souls' who were meant to be; it consoled me enormously that there were people like

Anya who seemed to understand the depth of my loss. When I wasn't visiting my grief counsellor, going robot-like through the motions of day-to-day life, or holed up at home re-reading Justin's letters, I would meet with close friends who were prepared to listen and let me talk. The party girl had completely fizzled out of me; I preferred friends one-on-one. Anything more left me feeling totally depleted.

Running, paradoxically, gave me some energy. Initially I'd reached for running shoes merely as a way to escape the emptiness of my house, but the routine of my long runs began to acquire a seductive, addictive pull. As I mourned, I would run, and run, and run. It was a fantastic way to clear my head and I found it hard to stop. I'd always been naturally sporty, but now I was emulating Justin who would always push me further when we would train together. He would always say, 'Pain is good, pain is good,' and that became my mantra when I'd go sprinting up a hill, pushing myself through a pain barrier until it did almost feel good. Without quite realising it was happening, I became exceedingly fit. What do they say? What doesn't kill you only makes you stronger.

But still, the memories of Justin that haunted me during those months were like a slow, cruel death. Almost anything could trigger a memory, especially when I was out in the natural world, when my mind would float back to the halcyon months we had together before he died. I was always my happiest when I was in nature, and when

I had been with Justin, I had been the happiest of all. There was nothing we had liked more than to go hiking, camping, skiing, cycling or running together.

One of the reasons I love to hike is because you have conversations when walking that you don't have anywhere or at any other time. It was like that for Justin and me. We loved being at the back of the pack where we'd yarn for hours about past experiences, our favourite recipes, hiking trips we wanted to take in the future with our children, memorable travel destinations and, one of our favourite topics, 'scariest encounters in nature'.

One weekend shortly after our love affair commenced, I'd arranged a long weekend hiking in the Grampians with a large group of friends, many of whom hadn't been hiking before. Justin and I couldn't believe the emails and telephone calls that came in the week before we were due to leave, asking questions that seasoned hikers could barely comprehend.

On the morning of the hike, he and I stared in amazement at the amount of gear our friends were planning to carry up the mountain for three days. Both of us were carrying the bare minimum; not for nothing was I nicknamed 'The Luggage Nazi'. Four hours into our hike, sure enough, all those who had ignored our advice about luggage were now struggling up the hill. Justin would quietly take their excess items and continue to climb.

He helped those who needed it, then sat down with someone else to bandage a badly blistered foot. He never reminded inexperienced hikers that they had been advised to 'walk their boots in'; instead, he was always patient, generous and kind, and I loved him for that. I knew that for a seasoned mountaineer like him, this was kindergarten stuff.

I also loved how Justin would tease me on our bush walks. When I go hiking, it's all about practicality; beauty and fashion go out the window. Justin would say, '*Ma folle fée*, one moment you look so ravishing and elegant, but when you go hiking, you look like a troll … that's why I love you'.

Justin and I were a team when it came to cooking around the campfire. I ardently believed that there was no need to compromise just because we were cooking alfresco and he completely agreed. We both adored cooking! Justin had a few specialties—seafood bouillabaisse and spaghetti vongole—and I had mine. We never fought in the kitchen or around a campfire; in fact, our tent became like a second home.

Even sitting at home in Melbourne with a glass of wine eating a delicious meal we had cooked together, we loved to turn our minds to the adventures we had ahead of us. We were planning to cycle around France on our bikes, living in our tent and cooking delicious food on our Trangia camping stove. We'd go hiking, just the two of us, in the Royal National Park south of Sydney and run races, naked, at the end of our trail, swimming nude in the ocean, delirious with exhaustion and hours of intimacy.

The fact that we were so evenly matched increased our enjoyment of all this activity immensely. Early in our relationship, we headed to Mt Hotham to go skiing for a long weekend. Because it was August and cold, we decided to ditch our tents and book a hotel suite complete with fireplace and jacuzzi!

After so many years of talking to each other about our skiing prowess, our favourite skiing destinations, the best snow we'd ever skied on, the falls we'd had and our experiences of ski seasons in France, we both began to fear that we had perhaps overstated our ability. As we took the ski lift for the first run of the day, we were both insisting, 'You go first. No no, you go first ... really ... you go.' Wouldn't it be embarrassing if one of us was not so advanced after all?

We needn't have worried. I was certainly impressed with Justin's level of skiing; in fact, I couldn't find him on the slopes most of the time. I would ski down and spot him in mid-air jumping off a cliff or out of a tree, or doing a triple somersault or a star jump. Bloody show-off!

My competitive streak kicked in and I took him on, and we'd entertain ourselves for hours, seeking out the ultimate runs off-piste. This meant crossing ridges, often taking off our skis and hiking to find places where no one else had been before. We loved being in the snow, laughing like kids as we pounded each other with snowballs, and always egging each other on for 'one more' last run.

But as the cliffs got higher, and the trees became bigger, and Justin's experiences with extreme skiers in Chamonix began to tell, my competitiveness waned. Not only a show-off, but also a madman!

Ten months after Justin's death, I decided to throw myself into organising a three-day hike for a dozen friends in the national park at Wilsons Promontory in Victoria. The hike was going to be hard and I gave all my friends fair warning to get fit. There were going to be ten of us, including Paddy and Nato, who were flying in for the weekend by light plane. Anya couldn't make it; she was attending a wedding in Sydney. I was delighted by my friends' response to the proposed hike and felt mildly recharged.

When we finally set out as a group in early October, I tended to hike along with Paddy and Nato and the three of us laughed a lot as we swapped stories. Paddy and Nato had always made me laugh; as a result, I felt the lightest I had been in months. I was back in nature, where I was always happiest, and surrounded by the love of friends.

Towards the hike's end, our friend Brett decided to take a shortcut back and head home early. Hours later, when we all reached the car park and Brett's car was still there, I became worried. More so, when I discovered Brett's mobile phone wasn't answering.

Paddy and Nato told me to stop worrying and, as a diversion, invited me to come along in their light plane to Canberra where we were all headed for business the next day. I declined and, still worried and a little preoccupied, helped them push the plane onto the tarmac at the nearby aerodrome. I hugged and waved the two of them goodbye and arranged to meet for lunch the following day.

That night, still unable to reach Brett on his mobile, I slept fitfully and woke at 5 am, convinced there would be a message waiting for me with an explanation. There was nothing. But still I felt sick in the stomach with worry, sensing simply that something was not right.

I caught my plane to Canberra and checked my phone for messages when I disembarked. Sure enough, my mobile was flashing. Not one, but 21 messages! My skin prickled, my blood went cold. Brett was fine, I heard, but Nato and Paddy's plane had crashed. Paddy was dead; Nato was seriously injured.

I went to the bathroom and vomited. The horror was starting all over again.

In November 1996, Nato's younger twin siblings, Deuchar and Tamsin, had died and now, six years later, we were burying 35-year-old Paddy and Nato was waging a ferocious battle to stay alive with horrific burns sustained in the plane crash. Both his legs had been amputated and the doctors were recommending that one arm, seriously infected, also be removed. I couldn't begin to imagine Nato and his family's pain and grief—

having three children who had been in tragic plane accidents was just too horrific to comprehend. On one of my hospital visits, I found Nato upright in bed, heavily bandaged and just as heavily drugged. He was practically unrecognisable—a huge, fit man withered to a stick with eyes like angry coals.

'Hello Nato,' I said softly as I approached his bedside. I could see his heart monitor start flickering furiously. 'Nato, I've been thinking about you so much, all your friends in Melbourne are thinking about you, we love you so much.' I leaned forward to stroke his bandaged arm.

Before I could even touch Nato, his face contorted in fury and his words came out like spit. 'Don't you say you love me! Stop being so condescending! I'm not doing a good job! I'm in *pain!* This is *hell*, do you hear me? *Hell.*'

This wasn't the Nato I had laughed with on the Wilsons Promontory hike; this wasn't the Nato who had waved me goodbye. I was face-to-face with a tormented soul and there was no human comfort I could bring to him. When I pulled out a gift I had brought with me— a photograph of all his friends in Melbourne gathered in a group to wish him a speedy recovery, Nato's heart monitor went wild. He collapsed back on his pillows, clenched in agony and stared at me as if he hated me more than life itself.

Shaken, I walked out of the ward on the flimsiest pretext and retched in the car park, too frightened to return and sit with my wounded and distressed friend. I felt insanely selfish. I knew what I was enduring was nothing compared to what Nato was going through. In fact, I was finding it difficult to take in anything at all. So much had happened and I felt unable to process anything properly.

Nato went in and out of consciousness for another two weeks until, on 22 December 2002, he died. I attended the funeral, held on a hot summer's day at the family cemetery on the Davy farm. It felt like only yesterday that we had all stood in the same place farewelling Nato's younger brother and sister. Like everyone else that day, I was struck dumb with grief. I had attended Tamsin and Deuchar's funeral; then Dave Englert's; then Justin's, then Paddy's, now this. I was completely numb as I went through the ritual of meeting and greeting old friends. Anya was there and we hugged each other wordlessly; it was a lot to take in. The only thing I can remember thinking as I drove home alone the day after the funeral was, 'Where have all my beautiful friends gone? What's happening to my life?'.

After the funeral, I couldn't be by myself. I suffered recurrent panic attacks, feeling as if all the air was being squeezed out of my lungs, convinced that I was going to die. I couldn't sleep. I couldn't concentrate on anything. I couldn't hold a conversation.

I couldn't live alone either. I had trouble carrying out even the most routine tasks, so I moved in with Pete and John. I saw a trauma counsellor weekly, took medication and occasionally had moments of clarity when I didn't think the car in which I was moving was going to crash, or the lift that I was taking was going to plummet downwards and smash into pieces with me inside.

A year after *Mon Amour* had died, I was exhausted from the effort of living life. Something had to give, I kept thinking, something had to change.

CHAPTER FIVE
MYNAH BIRDS & MONSOONS IN SERENDIP

Before Paddy died, he gave me a very precious gift: a ticket out of Australia in the form of Geoffrey Dobbs, hotelier extraordinaire. Geoffrey, who owned some of Sri Lanka's most beautiful boutique hotels and villas, known collectively as the Taprobane Collection, was looking for someone with a flair for cuisine and an interesting assortment of recipes to revitalise his hotels' fare. Paddy met him at a wedding in Galle, south of Colombo, following Justin's death, and recommended me to the flamboyant entrepreneur as just the person to take culinary command of his empire. During our brief romance, Paddy had raved about every dish I put before him, so it hadn't been difficult for him to wax lyrical about my talents in the kitchen.

'You look terrible Lobby, bloody terrible, you've got to get away,' he had told me bluntly when we'd met for dinner in Melbourne on his return. He pulled from his briefcase *Adventures of a Collector*, a book that he'd been reading by Lord Alistair McAlpine.

'In five years' time, do you want to pick up a book like this and think, I'd like to see some of the places he's seen? Or do you want to pick it up and think, yep, I've been there, seen this, experienced that?'

It was July 2002 when Paddy made this speech, and I was barely getting through what had so far been the worst seven months of my life. I knew Paddy was right— I needed a radical change. So I contacted Geoffrey Dobbs in Sri Lanka and when other mutual friends put in a strong word on my behalf, Geoffrey agreed to hire me on my terms whenever I felt ready. My network of friends, as always, did not let me down.

It took me six more months however, and Paddy and Nato's deaths, before I finally plucked up the courage to leave Australia. After months of panic attacks, grief counselling and a lot of tears alone at home, I knew I had to make a try at something positive. I also had to just 'let go', resign my job, pack my bags and confront my fear of flying. Somewhat nervously I climbed aboard a jumbo, farewelled my family and, on 17 January 2003, departed Australia for the Sri Lankan capital, Colombo.

When I boarded my flight, I felt an enormous sense of relief mixed with my trepidation about flying. I had just seen my mother, father, sister and my darling school friend Prue weep as they bade me farewell, but I had been largely silent.

Thank god, I'm out of here, I thought. I'm going somewhere where no one knows me. I can start again and do whatever I want. No more telephone calls from friends asking me how I am. No more, 'No seriously Lib, are you all right, tell me honestly, how are you doing?'.

I was tired of talking about it. For months before boarding that flight, I had become increasingly introverted, turning in on myself and literally, physically hunching over my chest as if guarding my heart. I yearned to start feeling alive again.

When I disembarked on Colombo's airport tarmac in the dead of night, a muggy tropical heat instantly enveloped me and I was hit by the smell of musky incense and tropical flowers. The hairs on my arm prickled with excitement. I had no idea what lay ahead, but I was very glad to have arrived. All I had was an address, a name and a telephone number.

I dialled the number and a foreign voice in broken English told me to jump in a taxi—'I will be waiting, madam'. After 30 minutes humming through the dark, I was ringing a bell at the entrance of a house. A man, all smiles, answered the call and ushered me past a fishpond into a house with large open-plan reception rooms. I later learned the house was designed by world-renowned Sri Lankan architect Geoffrey Bawa. I was led down a corridor to a bedroom with a four-poster bed, mosquito net and whirling ceiling fan. A tumbler and bottle of water stood on the bedside table. Through my open windows came the strong, lush scent of flowers. I felt instantly at home and totally charmed by my surroundings. I fell into bed and slept.

When I rose, my new friend, Gooneratne, laid a table for breakfast and shortly thereafter put papaya with lime, toast and tea before me and announced the imminent arrival of a Mr Namal.

Mr Namal? I was none the wiser, but waited patiently on the verandah under a fan and began to read my *Lonely Planet* guide to Sri Lanka as squirrels scurried up trees all around me.

Population: 20 million, about the same as Australia. Size: 433 kilometres long, 244 kilometres wide, roughly the same area as Tasmania or Ireland. Two monsoon seasons (May–August and October–January). About 2500 elephants still roaming wild. Alarming deforestation. Three main population groups: the majority Sinhalese who are mainly Buddhist; the Hindu Tamils comprising roughly one-fifth of the population; and the Muslim Sri Lankans who number one in ten.

Shortly after noon, having acquainted myself with the housekeeper, Leila, a toothless granny with a long silver plait who did not speak English and swept leaves with gusto, Mr Namal made an appearance. To my surprise, this man in crushed white linen and groovy sunglasses, speaking English at a hundred miles a minute, was not much older than me. Handsome, and wreathed in smiles, he seemed to talk in exclamation marks. 'Fantastic! You're here! We are going to open a coffee shop! I have so many ideas! Come, let me show you!'

He shepherded me next door to another superb Bawa-designed home with whirring fans and a tropical courtyard filled with an abundance of fragrant frangipani trees. Namal and I (having swiftly dispensed with formalities) talked about Mr Geoffrey's plans to open a city cafe on this site. I immediately imagined something very Sydney white damask tablecloths, olive oil in bowls on the table and so on—but before anything could solidify in my jet-lagged brain, Namal whisked me away to show off his city.

We jumped in one of hundreds of three-wheeler taxis (or *tuk-tuks*) zipping down the main road and careened down pot-holed city roads, narrowly missing buses, taxis, cars and pedestrians. The metropolis whirled past in a frenzied blur of colour, smells and noise. The rushing stopped only for a few concentrated visits to colourful and crazy fruit and vegetable markets, kitchen appliance stores and linen suppliers where friendly-looking locals emerged from the depths of tiny shops to answer all our questions. My new life in Sri Lanka had begun as it was to continue—full pelt—but at this early stage, I just felt jet-lagged. Namal suddenly announced, 'You be so tired! Too tired! You go home now! You sleep!'.

It was true. I had been in the country less than 24 hours and had barely had time to take in the completely different lifestyle and pace of this Asian country. I was overwhelmed by a vivid sense of the metropolis being awake and palpably alive. People covered in saris and smiles glided down the city's ramshackle streets as if promenading down Parisian boulevards. I was curious and enchanted, all at the same time, but all I wanted just then was to be horizontal with a pillow over my head.

A week later, Namal and I had slipped into a topsy-turvy routine of shopping and scouting for equipment and stock, interrupted only by a surprise whirlwind visit by Geoffrey's 80-year-old mother, Marie, her older sister, Bets, and their friend Mary, all three of them with a penchant for gin and tonics. Before even meeting Geoffrey, I was beginning to build a picture of my new boss—colourful, eccentric, and possibly just a little bit nutty?

Finally, I rose one morning for breakfast and noticed the breakfast table set for two. Gooneratne announced that Mr Geoffrey had arrived at midnight (all inbound Colombo flights did) and was soundly asleep in his bedroom. I was to meet the man himself at last. I instantly felt apprehensive, nervous about meeting the author of the steady stream of emails that had been popping up in my inbox for the last week. Fortunately, Namal arrived before my uneasiness could build, and next minute, there was Geoffrey himself—a big, curly-haired, tanned and friendly looking man, wearing a shirt emblazoned with 'Ceylon Elephant Polo 2002'. He extended a hand with a booming 'G'day!', which left me slightly stunned and suddenly lost for words.

But I needn't have worried; Geoffrey was not one for small talk. Within seconds, he was peeling the shell off his boiled egg, attacking a pile of toast and assailing me with questions. 'So Libby, what's news? What plans have you and Namal hatched?' He'd throw his tea down his throat and bellow, 'Gooneratne, more tea! More milk!'.

I would open my mouth to say something and he'd interrupt. 'Right, we've got elephant polo on the thirteenth, (hang on, that was less than four weeks away),

'I'm thinking a sit-down dinner for 60 for the first night? Then a sit-down lunch the following day for all the teams. What do you think? What should we have for starters?'

Again, I would open my mouth to reply, but he'd be off again. 'And what do you think of my cafe, huh? I want it open in time for the polo?'

I'd nod warily, making a polite effort to disguise my disbelief at such an unlikely prospect. Geoffrey sailed on. 'What sort of menus, do you think? We must have the best coffees this side of the Suez, of course. And health, we've got to do health! What do you think about beetroot and orange juice? Got to have fresh juices and soups! I'm a great fan of soups. What do you think? One hot, one cold?'

'I think …' But he was off again.

'No sandwiches, I don't think sandwiches. Do you agree?' As I would make to answer, Geoffrey would dab his chin with a napkin and call for Gooneratne to bring the Marmite.

This stranger, rattling away faster than a Tokyo train, was making Mr 'You! Be! Coming! Now! With! Me! Namal' look comatose by comparison. He was also my new boss in a very higgledy-piggledy foreign land. My head was beginning to spin, but Geoffrey was off again. 'You need to tell me how much it's going to cost to set up the cafe?'

His statements, I noticed, inevitably turned into questions that I needed to address. Finally, driven by desperation, I managed to get a word in.

'Well Geoffrey, there's absolutely nothing for the cafe except a sink, so we've got a way to go. We've got to get ovens, cupboards, shelving, a second sink, a dish-washing rack …' I started to tick off a list.

'Okay, okay,' Geoffrey said straight away. 'Get the carpenter in, show me the drawings, let's get moving … I want it open for the elephant polo!'

'Why don't Namal and I come up with a list of everything we need and then I'll tell you how much it's going to cost,' I replied quickly.

Geoffrey nodded, beaming, pleased that I seemed to be coming round. 'Okay, okay. So tell me, what do you think of my house? What do you think of my shop?' By now, we had abandoned breakfast and were walking around to the shop next door, where Geoffrey picked up some fabric samples on a table at the entrance, studied them briefly, and flung them dismissively on to the table. 'Namal—I told you, this isn't the right sample! This is completely WRONG. I told you I want 100 per cent cotton!'

I almost jumped out of my skin, while Namal opened his mouth to begin explaining. But Geoffrey was on a roll.

'And what about this floor?' As he scuffed the floor with his deck shoes you could see his blood pressure rise 'I asked for polished concrete. This is crap, absolute crap. Tell them to do it again! Just ridiculous!'

Welcome to Sri Lanka, I thought, let the fun begin.

Within days of meeting Geoffrey, who no sooner arrived than sped off to tour his various properties on the island, I realised I needed help. The elephant polo tournament, which Geoffrey initially visualised as a sporting joust with picnic hampers on a beach, had mutated into a monster celebration. This would involve private dinners for the Sri Lankan Prime Minister and his party, glamorous dinners for the competitors at Geoffrey's various hotels and villas and gourmet barbecue lunches on the beach. A gala dinner finale was also planned for 150 people on Taprobane Island; the jewel in Geoffrey's crown of sumptuously rustic holiday locations was the most exclusive spot in Galle, the 'Riviera' of the teardrop island of Sri Lanka.

I wasn't merely the chef—I was cook, cleaner and event manager for a four-day sporting event sprung, it seemed to me, from a mind that was possibly unhinged. Who had ever heard of elephant polo, for goodness' sake?

Namal gave me a crash course on what to expect: six teams (with three players and a reserve on each) from Scotland, Australia, Hong Kong, India, Thailand and Nepal, were shortly to descend on Serendip's shores to challenge the Sri Lankans for the Ceylon Elephant Polo 2003 trophy. I listened, amused, as Namal explained the rules of the game:

1. Each game is played by three players per team on a field that is roughly the size of a football pitch.

2. The game consists of two seven-minute playing periods called chukkas with an interval of 15 minutes between each chukka.

3. There are no restrictions as to the height, weight or sex of the elephants.

4. No elephant may lie down in front of the goal.

5. An elephant may not pick up the ball with its trunk during play.

6. Gentlemen may hold the mallets in their right hands only; ladies may use both hands.

7. The following acts constitute a foul: hooking the opponent's stick, deliberately crossing in front of an elephant when the opponent is moving with the ball, standing on the ball, backing or going forward over a ball to stop a player reaching the ball, intentionally hitting another player, elephant or referee with a stick.

8. At close of play, sugarcane, bananas or rice balls shall be given to the elephants and a cold beer or soft drink to the elephant drivers (*mahouts*), but not vice versa.

Twelve elephants (to be rotated among the teams) were in training for the big event and a dozen *mahouts* were poised to join the international visitors aboard the elephants. The *mahouts* sit in front of the players atop the elephants because without them, the elephants don't move, thus killing any chance of goal scoring. With the *mahouts* egging the elephants on, usually by tickling them behind the ears, the players aim to hit the ball through goal posts. Thousands of spectators were expected to arrive to watch the 2003 polo spectacle and two commentators, one English, one Sri Lankan, were primed to whip the crowd into a frenzy.

Now all I had to do, single-handedly it appeared, was arrange a few bits and pieces. Let's see, there was the tournament schedule to organise; including player accommodation and hospitality; VIP arrivals and departures; transportation of chairs, tables and crockery from Colombo to the tournament site (still unseen); a few national flags, megaphones, loudspeakers and referee whistles to whip up; and elephant mounting stands to be erected. Then, of course, there was my chief task, which was to devise mouthwatering menus for the myriad functions Geoffrey was planning over the course of the four days, to purchase the stock and prepare the meals themselves, as well as organise people to serve and pour drinks for the guests.

Anya, still in mourning for Paddy, was due to arrive in Sri Lanka in a few days to visit me. We were now firm friends and felt a strong connection. We'd both lost our lovers, so we completely understood one another. In fact, we'd often comment that one of Paddy's most valuable legacies was our friendship.

Perhaps Anya would be able to help me with the polo event, but I didn't want to bank on it; I knew she was suffering terribly and might not be able to rally to the call.

I needed more help and thought of Andrea, the sous-chef from my Lobby Lobster days, who I knew was between jobs.

I rang her and, in true Andrea form, my friend agreed to help, unfazed by the lack of salary and delighted at the thought of an adventure in exotic climes. She suggested that her boyfriend, Charlie, also at a loose end, might be happy to tag along. Charlie was funny, fit, entertaining and talented with a camera and an acoustic guitar. I was delighted and knew I could easily put him to good use. Almost overnight I had my very own catering unit and my panic began to subside. Anya (I hoped) and I would have 16 days to prepare for Geoffrey's showcase event, then Andrea and Charlie would arrive just in time to help during the tournament week itself. And then, out of the blue, popped my new fabulous friend, Soos, whom I had recently met through Geoffrey. Soos was from the UK, visiting for the tourist season, and happened to be a talented stylist—perfect, I thought, to decorate our different party venues.

Within days, Anya landed at Colombo Airport weighed down with sandwich toasters and muffin tins, pine nuts, kalamata olives, crispbreads and endless other things I had begged her to bring. We dropped everything and hugged each other ecstatically. Happy as I was to see her however, I couldn't help but notice how sad she looked. With a start, I realised how Sri Lanka, despite its frustrations, had already begun to work its magic on me.

For one thing, everything I did in my new hot and humid hometown was so energy-sapping that I found it much easier to get to sleep than I had for a long time. I would whisper my ruminations to Justin last thing at night, the honking of taxis and buses gradually fading in the distance, and notice with giddy relief that a few hours had passed that day when I hadn't experienced that familiar stab to the chest each time I remembered something he had said or something we had done together. By contrast, Anya was still in the early stages of grief.

I was relieved to throw myself into planning an event that would guarantee me little time to think about anything personal if I was to make my new boss proud. I was constantly amused by Geoffrey, who would assume a different silly accent every time he called—his non-stop energy and enthusiasm proved infectious. I was being paid a paltry wage, but I was relishing the freedom and flexibility Geoffrey allowed—my place in his hospitable home and the opportunity to immerse myself in another culture. I was happy, in short, to give it all my best shot.

But the realities were daunting. Headquartered in the house where we ate and slept, the 'office' consisted of a battle-axe computer and a rusty fax machine with Internet access courtesy of a cafe around the corner. Most frustrating of all was the Valium everyone in Sri Lanka seemed to be taking and the lack of respect for deadlines (so different to the world of advertising in which I had worked for years). I was swiftly learning that no one ever said 'no' to a request—but that this didn't necessarily signify a 'yes'. I was learning that the local response to almost any request was to waggle one's head accommodatingly, confusing the hell out of foreigners like me. I would find myself puce with frustration, asking again and again, 'Do you mean yes, or do you mean no? Yes? No?'

The faxes and emails from Geoffrey, meanwhile, piled up at an alarming rate. Ideas. Suggestions. Commandments. There would be recipes for tomato summer puddings or tips for whipping up borscht or preparing a beetroot and vodka shot. Occasionally, he would stroll in unexpectedly and start peppering Anya and me with questions. Haphazardly, his vision for his boutique hotels, and Sri Lankan tourism in general, began to emerge. No idea was too big, no vision too grandiose. An elephant polo tournament was the least of it.

While Geoffrey thought big, Anya and I got on with the more pressing tasks on our checklist, including choosing suitable wines with which to impress the tournament guests. As Chivas Regal was one of the event's sponsors, the company's wine representative, 'Wickie', duly called by with a selection of French and Australian wines for us to sample. Anya, Wickie and I tasted each in a bid to shortlist the best for Geoffrey's approval. Several glasses later, Anya and I were teaching Wickie Australian phrases like 'up your clacker', as we clinked glasses. We were a very merry trio when we eventually called it a night.

A few nights later, with the arrival of the international teams imminent, I escaped the hustle and bustle to attend the Buddhist festival of the moon, Navam Perahera. Anya was unwell, so I went solo by *tuk-tuk*, my driver struggling to make his way through the throngs to the temple where the festival procession was due to start. I could feel the excitement in the air and, shivering with anticipation, was heartily glad to be a part of it. After weeks of thinking of nothing else but recipes and provision lists, it was a delight to be swept up in a throng of masked revellers drumming furiously behind a cavalcade of bejewelled elephants.

Grandstands lined the streets, fire dancers leapt through the crowds and monks in ornate headgear played various percussion instruments. I was a pale-faced solitary female in a crowd of steaming Sri Lankans, but instead of feeling an outsider, I felt a sense of belonging, even bliss. The Perahera crowd seemed to welcome me unconditionally as we all marched, swayed and were swept along together. For 90 throbbing minutes, I felt myself transported by the pulsating drums, dancing flames and sea of sequinned costumes.

Then, suddenly, a massive electrical storm interrupted the revelry. The heavens opened and, in a flash, the festivities were washed out. I waded home in shin-high water, drenched and bedraggled, slipping into bed, glad to have been privy to Buddha's wild, wet party.

'*Mon Amour,*' I whispered to Justin as I hit my pillows, 'you would have loved to be there'.

The first day of the 2003 International Elephant Polo tournament finally dawned. So far, my little crew, with Andrea and Charlie in full swing, had safely met and accommodated the tournament players in Geoffrey Dobbs's various habitats in and around the picturesque town of Galle. The VIP seating was in place, commentators were primed and villagers were beginning to throng to the beach at Weligama Bay, the playing field for the tournament, close to Taprobane Island. The elephants were standing by, saddled-up, watered and tethered, and the *mahouts* were ready for action. There was just one problem— the first day of the tournament boasted a full moon, resulting in high tides that completely washed away the tournament's playing fields.

Disaster! It was no use trying to play in the early morning or late afternoon as originally planned: waves would wash away the goalposts and the balls would be submerged in sandy sludge.

Teams had flown in from all over the world, the weather was perfect, and hundreds of excited spectators waited, national flags fluttering from every available pole or post. Referees were armed with shiny new whistles— and now a completely new schedule of events, with the poor elephants having to play at noon when the sun was highest and hottest. With the changing itinerary, Andrea, Anya, Charlie and I found ourselves even busier, if that was possible. Geoffrey would announce more dinners and new VIPs with alarming regularity and the four of us and our confused, muddled helpers would run around under the Serendip sun in 35°C heat and 80 per cent humidity, serving canapés and filling beers until everyone was thoroughly sozzled.

Driving with the girls one evening from Weligama Bay to one of Geoffrey's exclusive boutique hotel in the hills above Galle, loaded with provisions for yet another dinner, I suddenly thought of Justin. A memory of us sitting happily around a campfire swept over me with frightening intensity. Oh Juz, why can't you be here to be part of this? I thought.

Before I knew it, I found myself in a flood of tears, unable to stop. Our driver, concerned and uncertain, slowed down almost to a halt. Andrea, giant punchbowl filled with fruit balancing on her knees, ordered him to keep moving. We were late and she was worried about the dinner, but when she turned to me, her fine blonde hair a frizz after a long day of catering to a thousand whims, her face was etched with concern.

I just couldn't pretend I was okay one minute more. Suddenly, not even the ceaseless activity could distract me from my loneliness. Anya held my hand; Andrea patted my knee with her one spare hand and for 40 minutes, until we arrived at the hotel, I wept. Emerging from the vehicle, wrung out but partially comforted, I walked into the kitchen.

Immediately, it became clear that we had a minor disaster on our hands: the hotel staff had forgotten to defrost the prepared pea and lettuce soup planned for the entrée and guests were already beginning to arrive.

Andrea and I spent the next ten minutes hacking the soupy-green blocks of ice into chunks small enough to squeeze into the one pot that would fit in the minuscule microwave. My emotional turmoil was immediately subsumed by yet another minor domestic drama.

'When in doubt, divert' is one of my favourite entertaining mottos, so we decided to get creative with the presentation of the soup, coming up with all sorts of garnishes and means of presenting the below-par appetiser. We upped the energy, hilarity and entertainment value for the dinner and *voila*! It seemed to work because both Geoffrey and his guests beamed, replete, at the end of it all.

As the tournament began in earnest, my crew and I began to familiarise ourselves with the different national teams. There was James Manclark from Scotland, who was the initiator of the colourful, crazy carnival, ably seconded by his glamorous wife, Patricia. A former Olympic bobsleigh champion, Manclark had become bored with his icy sport and graduated to the equally risky pursuit of motorcar racing before he tried a traditional bout of polo and got hooked. Then, he thought it might be fun to have countries competing against one another astride the elephants. Why?

'Because one can,' Manclark would announce triumphantly to no-one in particular.

With his good friend, Jim Edwards, owner of the world famous Nepalese resort Tiger Tops, Manclark convinced a network of their friends around the globe to indulge his idea. Compatriots Peter Prentice and the Duke of Argyll played with Manclark for the Chivas Regal team, flying Scotland's colours, while Edwards played for Nepal, joined by his son Kristjan and Kristjan's girlfriend, Hattie.

Geoffrey had party animal Dominic Moynihan and ex-army colonel Raj Kalaan and his wife, Sunny, on his Sri Lankan team; when the three of them weren't bickering about obscure past hurts, each exhibited an unrivalled keenness to take the winner's trophy. Excitement and enthusiasm were the order of the day, with passion raging white-hot as commentators urged the spectators to yelp, boo, whistle, clap and even throw bananas.

The so-called 'action' was more of a plod, but even so, with all my rushing around I barely had time to take it in. Riders, resplendent in national colours, seemed mostly to be limply hanging on, waiting with mallets in hand, while the wild-eyed *mahouts* tickled and prodded their charges to little avail. Occasionally, when an elephant moved and a rider would take a swing, the patient crowd would burst into a roar of delight, and then fall into silence until the next successful thwack!

My catering unit, meanwhile, was wading endlessly back and forth through low-tide water from the

Weligama beach to Taprobane Island, with boxes of ice, chairs and tables on their heads.

It was just another day in paradise and after a round of play-offs, the Sri Lankan team, under the captainship of Geoffrey Dobbs, became elephant polo champions of Ceylon for the second year in a row. Geoffrey was delighted, cheeks cherry-red after an afternoon astride his elephant, hoisting his trophy for the local press photographers. I breathed a sigh of relief. This long, muggy nightmare of endless revelry was, finally, slowly drawing to a close.

Then, unexpectedly, I heard my name being called over the loudspeaker. 'Will Miss Libby Southwell please come to the presentation platform ...'

I felt instant frustration. The gala ivory ball for 150 was almost upon us and I still had a million things to do; I was also sunburnt and exhausted from carrying equipment all day long, and I looked a sight. My shorts and singlet were covered in grease, chocolate and tomato stains; my fingernails were crusted with pastry and my sweaty, smelly auburn locks were clamped underneath a filthy cotton scarf. This was no time for me to have to meet with someone else Geoffrey wanted to impress. For goodness sake, I thought irritably, what did he want now?

As I approached the podium where the trophies had just been presented, I suddenly realised that everyone who had been on stage, including the winning players and the Sri Lankan Prime Minister himself, appeared to be waiting patiently for me. Sure enough, I was duly presented with the Dominic Moynihan Cup for 'Best Performance Off the Field'. The Prime Minister said something encouraging, the crowd clapped politely and the photographers' cameras clicked.

Through it all, ridiculous thoughts whirred through my head: What about the hummus? Where the hell are Andrea's feta and tomato tarts? Dazed, I looked around at the others on stage and caught my boss beaming with pride. I didn't know whether to laugh or cry.

Within minutes, my moment of glory had faded in the turmoil of dinner preparation. With less than two hours to go, we still hadn't finished draping the reception areas in creamy fabric for the party's ivory theme. The food stations were a shambles, the bar ice was melting and we couldn't wedge one more celery stick in either of the two fridges even with invocations to Buddha. The barbecue was belching coconut oil smoke, the vegetables were soggy, and the fireworks and flares had gone missing.

Anya was feeling sick, Andrea was in meltdown, even Charlie looked worried and everyone, absolutely everyone, was calling me on my mobile phone to sort out his or her various dramas. Then Geoffrey arrived and started bellowing, 'Where's the bar? Where are the decorations? We can't make compromises! Do you hear me? *We can't make compromises!*'

Somehow, we got through it, but even I don't know how. I just remember doing a million things at once, all night barking orders until the last guest was escorted away and I collapsed.

One of my last memories that night is of Geoffrey lifting a cevapcici to his mouth, taking a bite gingerly, and throwing his meat-impaled stick into the black of the night. 'This is *not* cevapcici,' he roared, well into his cups by now. 'You call this cevapcici? Well I tell you, it's NOT!'

The third of April Justin's birthday was the day in 2003 that Geoffrey happened to choose to host a cocktail party for British residents, mainly embassy people, in Colombo. Wiser by now, having realised I was much more than a mere cook for Taprobane's manic head honcho, I had already hired and trained a chef for the upcoming shindig which was to be held at the Colombo shop and adjoining cafe the same cafe that Geoffrey had wanted to open in time for the polo.

'I want the best food in Sri Lanka! The best canapés! No excuses, you just organise it. I'll be there at 8 o'clock; see you there!'

I sighed, tired of the criticisms, commands and ceaseless chorus of, 'I want, I want, I want'. What I wanted was to crawl into a hole and to never come out.

Since the polo event, we had only had one week's reprieve during which Anya got seriously sick with an ear infection, and then a series of dramas. Geoffrey had been forced to sack difficult staff and that had involved

mynah birds & monsoons in serendib

re-hiring and re-training an entire hospitality team for one of the villas. Then, huge tropical storms left another villa with a power blackout and that did nothing to endear the villa staff to our overseas visitors. Finally, making Geoffrey's proposed target to open the cafe was proving an ongoing challenge when construction and delivery deadlines were as slippery as mudslides in a monsoon.

On the morning of the cocktail party, we were finally set to officially open but I just couldn't muster the wherewithal to climb out of bed. Anya found me, surrounded by scrunched-up tissues, weeping inconsolably. I wanted Justin; I wanted to be somewhere else. Anya's eyes were huge as she took in my desolation, understanding completely what I felt. For my part, I didn't know how I was going to shower and dress, let alone host a cocktail party.

Somehow, we got through the work and then Geoffrey was there. 'Let's try some of the food! Oh, this is a bit crunchy! I don't like this,' and he'd move onto the next canapé. 'Hmmmm, this is good, but *oooh*, don't like this'.

An hour later, when less than half the expected guests arrived and about 25-dozen canapés still remained, I left the party to its own devices. By this stage, I was so sad I couldn't speak. I went to the courtyard of the house, switched off the lights and sat in the dark. But it wasn't long before I heard Geoffrey calling to all and sundry and no one in particular, 'Libby, anyone seen Libby? LIBBY! Where's Libby?'

Anya cornered him and let rip a torrent of grievances. 'Geoffrey, you just don't understand. Libby has been working so hard and you haven't thanked her ... not once! And Libby is so sad today; today is Justin's birthday and you just don't seem to care and we are sick of it.'

Then Anya was in tears too. I rushed out to comfort her and Geoffrey stood there, stuck for words. 'It's not fair, Geoffrey,' I said between gritted teeth, 'it's not fair'. 'I know it's not Libby,' Geoffrey replied at last, speaking unbelievably slowly. 'Look, I'm sorry. You've done so much! I will be forever indebted to you.'

We said we weren't working another day; Geoffrey agreed and fled to bed and we retired ourselves. That night both Anya and I, still trying to deal with our grief in the midst of madness, cried ourselves to sleep.

The next day, Geoffrey had left for another part of the island and, at last, Anya and I were free to have the sort of holiday that we so desperately needed.

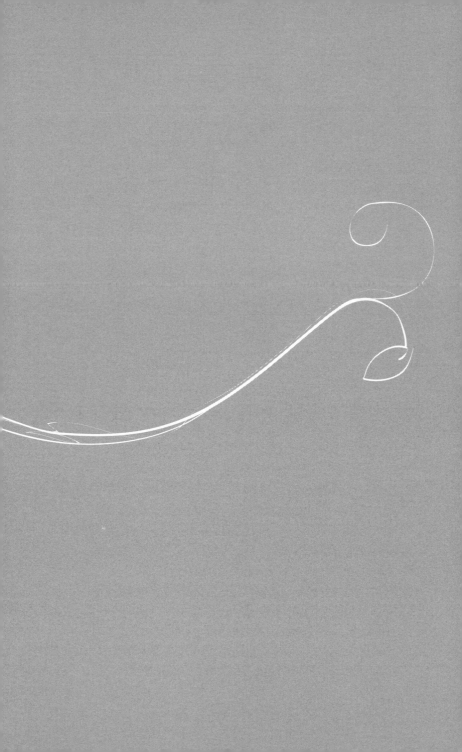

CHAPTER SIX
INDIA GOBBLES US UP

Initially, Anya and I set aside five weeks for rest and relaxation in Sri Lanka, but then we decided to also go to India, and after that possibly extend our holiday and travel to all the Asian countries about which we had read and often yearned to visit. Both of us had plenty of savings and I had the additional security of knowing that I had work with Geoffrey back in Sri Lanka whenever I chose to return. In the meantime, the tourism supremo had given me his blessing and a fistful of brilliant contacts.

First though, we took full advantage of Geoffrey's numerous properties on the Sri Lankan south coast and lolled around on golden beaches for ten days, then hired a driver and van and set off along the pockmarked, pot-holed, serpentine national highways to see the country further north.

Around Kandy and Nuwara Eliya in the central hill country we found life more rustic. We stayed in colonial-inspired guesthouses with high ceilings, expansive rooms and bursts of pink and orange foliage in manicured gardens. We'd wake in the morning in the lush, peaceful surrounds and hear no sound for hours except the chattering of birds. Once we'd acclimatised to the rhythms of each new place, we would venture forth to sightsee and browse through the village marketplaces close by.

One morning, as we scouted for accommodation in Nuwara Eliya, we noticed the growing excitement in the air. More locals than usual were hurrying to and fro, weighed down with parcels; the bazaars buzzed.

We asked a friendly shopkeeper what was going on. It turned out that April was the month of the Buddhist New Year, a time for cleansing and renewal. We discovered that family members bought each other new pots and pans for cooking; furniture for working and resting, and clothes to transform and rejuvenate them for the year ahead. As part of the celebration, families also got together to eat, drink and exchange gifts— rather like our Christmas.

Anya and I joined in the spirit of the happy occasion and gave each other small gifts of renewal (soaps for cleansing, a new diary for novel thoughts, fresh socks for hiking) and then joined a throng of pilgrims on the ascent to Adam's Peak, a sacred mountain famous as a goal of pilgrimage for Buddhists, Hindus and Muslims. At the summit is a large flat rock that bears the impression of an oversized human foot. The Buddhists believe this footprint is Buddha's, the Hindus think it is Shiva's and the Muslims consider it to be the footprint of Adam. All visitors were encouraged to begin the four-hour ascent at 2 am to reach the summit in time for sunrise.

Happy to do it the 'Lankan' way, Anya and I decided to go. We were excited at the thought of a steep, bracing walk, anticipating a beautiful dawn at the completion of our climb and a leisurely hike home in the glory of nature. We prepared like the seasoned hikers we were: thermal underwear, walking boots, fleeces, Gortex rain jacket, torches with spare batteries, even a medicine bag, just in case. Even before we arrived at the departure point however, we began to notice something strange. Lights sparkled everywhere in the darkness and we could distinctly hear music threading its way through the cool night air. As we approached, to our astonishment, we saw we were entering a sideshow alley!

Market stalls lined the path on either side and everywhere we looked hawkers peddled giant blow-up animals, bags of candy, temple flags, banners and carry bags in a profusion of colour and noise. The aroma of roasted peanuts wafted through the night air and as far as the eye could see, pilgrims in beanies, saris, turbans, dreadlocks or soft veils were stocking up on provisions for the climb. Children, about to make the ascent in a parent's arms, looked bewildered or sleepy. As Western hiking enthusiasts, Anya and I just looked completely out of place.

Taken aback but determined, with snacks and water bottles packed, we jostled through the crowd and began to climb the 5200 steps that led to the place where, it is said, Adam first set foot on earth when he was ejected from Paradise. As our knees creaked up this never-ending stairway, Anya and I were flabbergasted to find bare-footed geriatrics among our fellow travellers. This was, truly, the strangest 'hike' we'd ever been on in our life.

Everyone seemed to make it to the top regardless and when we reached the summit, more puffed out than we thought possible after a gruelling seven kilometres of stairs, we found ourselves squashed with at least a thousand pilgrims on a piece of rock the size of a tennis court. Anya and I had been looking forward to witnessing a spectacular sight from 'one of the most revered cathedrals of the human race'. Instead, we found ourselves fruitlessly craning over the tops of the same beanies, turbans, dreadlocks and veils that had accompanied us along the way. We didn't catch even a glimpse of the mountain's legendary sunrise.

According to my *Lonely Planet* travel guide, on this mountain, the sun casts a perfect shadow of the peak on the misty clouds down towards the coast, and then, as it rises, this shadow races back towards the peak, eventually disappearing into its base. Anya and I saw none of it, but we high-fived one another anyway, proud to have trod in Prince Siddharta's footsteps. For the next five days, however, neither of us could walk without flinching in pain and we cursed the gods.

Semi-recovered, we travelled on to the drier northeast of the Cultural Triangle and visited the ancient royal cities of Sinhalese civilisation. These are Anuradhapura and the slightly younger Polonnaruwa, both built more than 1000 years ago at the height of Buddhist culture during an age when Sri Lanka was known as Rajarata, or land of kings

We also visited the spectacular rock fortress of Sigiriya, built in the fifth century AD by one of King Dhatusena of Anuradhapura's sons, Kasyapa, who feared retribution after overthrowing his father. Since restored by archaeologists, Sigiriya is proudly labelled by Sri Lankans as the eighth wonder of the world and it's not an idle boast. We were enthralled, meandering through the ancient palace, and found ourselves enchanted by the design and engineering detail, the breathtaking art and beautiful landscaping.

We sped further north to Trincomalee, a superb beach oasis just below the Tamil Tiger-controlled northern province. There we sipped shandies with friends on their verandah and watched the swooping egrets, spoonbills, cormorants and storks compete with local fishermen for the catch of the day.

The Sri Lankan leg of our holiday slipped by in a pleasant blur of coastal swims interspersed with long treks by car into the hinterland. Lulled into torpor as we were chauffeured along, we passed ramshackle villages that were a blur of ceaseless noise, traffic and colour, occasionally rousing ourselves to burst into song. Often, seeing something strangely typical of Sri Lanka would set us off. We'd spy a father, a mother and two little girls with pigtails, all sitting together, calmly, on a one-seater motorcycle, chugging up a hill. Or, we'd spot a tattered billboard exhorting the populace to 'Drink Elephant Soft Drinks', with a beggar sitting below petitioning for more essential fare. Then, a shopkeeper shooing away a gaggle of wily monkeys feeding on a scrap heap or a signboard proclaiming '100% Fitness Gym' above a dingy, clapped-out shop through which we could spy a solitary enthusiast trying out a treadmill. A jeep would drive past, groaning under the weight of a small elephant and Anya and I would look at each other and start laughing and then perhaps begin a spontaneous duet. 'Summertime … and the living is easy. Fish are jumping, and the cotton is high …'

Anya and I loved Sri Lanka's madness. It was an infuriating and unpredictable place, but it burrowed its way into our hearts nevertheless. We savoured moments of gaiety and sometimes succumbed to rivers of tears. While I still mourned for Justin, I could also sense freedom beginning to stir inside me; for Anya however, there was mostly pain. Her anguish was often suppressed, but unexpected moments would set her off. She'd pick up a magazine, read a headline, and react. Then, after an outburst where she'd rail against the injustices, cruelties and hardships of the world, she would break into tears.

'I can't do this, I can't do this,' Anya would wail. Then she'd throw her head back and say with determination. 'No, enough. I can hear Paddy telling me I must go on.'

I could relate totally to Anya's pain. Ever since Paddy had introduced Anya and me, we had felt connected. Now, almost 18 months on, tragic circumstances had brought us closer together. We were able to comfort each other without unrealistic expectations. As the grief struck both of us at different times, we simply rode the roller coaster in tandem and supported one another. There was an understanding of what the other was going through that made it easy for both of us.

On this holiday, Anya was going through what I had suffered a year before. I remembered all too well what it had been like to struggle out of bed each morning. As the date of our departure for India approached and I saw how Anya was soldiering on through the sightseeing and travel, I suggested that she should just forget about visiting India. It was too painful, too much, especially given that she and Paddy had planned precisely the sort of trip we were about to make. They had bought and paid for tickets; meticulously researched their three-month itinerary, arranged visas and even half-packed their luggage. They were to have met Paddy's parents, sojourned together in France and then made their engagement official. It was to have been a gloriously romantic getaway.

The pair of them had been madly in love, and their relationship, like Justin's and mine, had been brilliant and all too brief. Anya and Paddy were practically all set to board their flight to Delhi when Paddy was killed. I couldn't help thinking, grimly, that the omens for India were not good.

Despite my reluctance, Anya was determined. We would go to India together and we would have the adventure we both wanted. But as we set off, she seemed immersed already in a fog. Before we even boarded our flight, she lost her wallet and a stash of cash; I found myself continually guiding her through a checklist as we negotiated various stages of our journey. Got your passport? Wallet? Camera? Where's your daypack? Do you need something to eat or drink? What about a hat?

Things didn't get any better during a 12-hour stopover at Bangkok airport when a long email Anya had been typing at an Internet cafe disappeared into the ether. It took only the littlest thing to tip her over the edge. By the time we arrived in Delhi's cacophony of colour, noise and 45°C heat, both she and I were wiped out.

Mustering some enthusiasm, we headed over for lunch with Sunny and Raj Kalaan, our elephant polo friends, where we were embraced with Indian hospitality and food. We ate up a storm, had a few beers, relished the air conditioning and after a short rickshaw ride home, collapsed in our hotel room. That evening, another polo player, Jaisal Singh of the Indian team, invited us for dinner and drinks. Enchanted by the exuberance of the occasion, Anya transformed into a butterfly. It was heart-warming to see the old Anya I knew and loved. Her determination to embrace India was admirable, yet I knew it was an ongoing effort for her.

By comparison, I was stronger and able to experience heady moments like the night of Jaisal's party. Jaisal's guests included politicians, film directors, writers, polo players and one breathtakingly beautiful 23-year-old model, Anjula Bias-Singh. Anjula was like the Paris Hilton of Delhi except that this sari-clad debutante had a master's degree rather than her own porn video. Educated in the United States, Anjula was as friendly and outgoing as she was beautiful, regularly invited by the media as a spokesperson on behalf of young Indian women. She and I took to each other immediately and were soon engrossed in conversation about Western versus Eastern culture. Then, before I knew it, she was insisting Anya and I move in with her for the duration of our Delhi stay. Holy Shiva! How lucky could a pair of Aussie girls get?

The next day, after a night filled with food, drink, great conversation and lots of fun, we took up Anjula's offer and checked out of our hotel. We left our luggage in her cosy two-bedroom apartment decorated in a mishmash of Bollywood-meets-suburban-Miami style, cooled down briefly in the one air-conditioned room the apartment boasted and ventured out again, somewhat refreshed. Within 60 seconds, we were broiling in the stupefying heat; to Anya especially, it felt like she was in meltdown.

They say that Delhi is an assault on your senses, and it's no exaggeration. Even the strongest, bravest or hardest heart cannot ignore the onslaught of human energy that bubbles, spits and careens through the shimmering streets of this humid metropolis.

For Anya, it was as if she had been lowered into Dante's inferno. She would totter bravely through the streets, shrinking as another beseeching, screeching beggar approached her, thrusting paper rupees into their hands until her purse was empty and then, close to tears, would look at me. No words would be exchanged; I could see that it was eating her up. I would hold her hand, squeeze it tight and on we would go to our next destination, rattling along in our three-wheeler in the noise, pollution and heat.

Both Anya and I loved the shopping and the markets. It took us into another world where we almost forgot about the reality of the environment around us—the colour, movement, noise and exotic smells. Time would totally disappear, allowing Anya brief moments to forget about her pain. We would scour the bazaars for wall hangings, antique saris and exotic jewellery and revel in the colonial architecture, the old Muslim quarters, the forts, palaces, shrines and cathedrals, the throbbing madness, the centuries of history, the sheer chaos of the place.

A few days later, Anya and I bade our Delhi princess farewell and climbed aboard a train to see the Taj Mahal at Agra. This train proved to have air conditioning that worked. More praise to Shiva! Agra, on the other hand, was a dry and dusty hellhole, five degrees hotter than Delhi with antiquated water coolers. Fortunately, the Taj Mahal looked as glamorous as the postcards, but not even our mutual excitement at seeing a world wonder first-hand could entice Anya to leave her bed for long. The heat was paralysing for both of us and Anya in particular was struggling. 'When we get to Agra, I'll feel better,' Anya had said, trying to convince herself. Now it was, 'When we get to Jaipur, I'll be fine.'

In fact, things continued to deteriorate. If we got the triumvirate of good fortune in one day—namely, an air-conditioned dwelling; a toilet unadorned by stale urine or leftover pooh; and a tasty meal that wasn't swimming in oil—we would consider ourselves extraordinarily blessed. On such a day, we would drink in every vista and relish each new experience in this incredible country.

But mostly, India was sapping the last bit of Anya's strength. I suggested on several occasions that we return to Delhi and that I put Anya on a plane to Australia. However, she kept insisting that she would feel better when she got to the next place ... and the next. I admired her determination—when I had experienced the worst of my grieving, all I'd wanted was comfort and familiarity. Here, we were very far away from both.

Our next stop was the city of Jaipur where we planned to splash out on ritzy accommodation—US$100 a night! First, however, we had a 12-hour train ride and we found ourselves on a station platform, surrounded by beggars, rubbish and crows, with nothing we dared to eat and what proved to be a four-hour wait to endure.

When an ancient steam locomotive finally puffed into view we discovered we were sharing our sleeping compartment with an extended family: two men on the top bunk, two women in the middle and four children on the bottom. This was a journey that would have tested the mettle of even the most seasoned and energetic traveller. For Anya, it was the last straw.

Many months later, Anya would tell me how she had felt in Jaipur—'desperate' was the word she kept using. The beauty and misery of India, she told me, had completely overwhelmed her in her vulnerable state. Moreover, she found it hard to accept that Paddy wasn't there with her to share what she was seeing. As a result, she hadn't really been able to appreciate anything. Someone remarked to her afterwards that India can 'gobble you up'; she had felt completely gobbled up.

It was obvious Anya had pushed herself far beyond what she could bear. So, back in Delhi, after lots of conversations and sleepless nights, we had a long talk and Anya decided it was time to go home and heal. As I waved goodbye at the airport, I felt compassion for my friend, but I also knew she would be all right, given time.

The next morning, I took a second-class train that wound its way northwards from the hot plains of Delhi to the cooler hilltop town of Shimla, on the southern border of the state of Himachal Pradesh. I was headed for mountain territory in the shadow of the Indian Himalayas and I was full of anticipation.

In Shimla, fate presented me with another precious gift in the form of Kamal, a mountain man from a nearby town who spoke excellent English and knew the region intimately. With Kamal as guide, I found a German couple, Det and Eve, to share the cost, and together we hired a jeep to begin our journey to India's northerly hill kingdoms. It wasn't long before our party of four found itself collectively holding our breath as we crawled across a succession of temporary suspension bridges. It was the beginning of several weeks of navigation across terrain that grew increasingly perilous, icy, barren and remote with periodic stops in villages for refreshment, rest and sleep. There were breathtaking hikes with snow-capped mountains for backdrops and numerous encounters with villagers, nomads and hospitable families with whom we'd swap stories and experiences. And, always, there was time for me to think.

One morning I awoke from a broken sleep, bodily sore and low in spirit. For almost six months after Justin's death my heart had physically hurt so that I was unable to lie on the left-hand side of my body to sleep. Now, many months later, the pain had returned and after dreaming fitfully about Justin and the mountains, I felt dangerously close to tears. I knew how much he would have loved all of this and I felt a desperate yearning for him to be there, right then, with me. The Indians have a philosophical way of shrugging gently with a 'What to do?' when faced with something painful but inevitable, and I could relate. What to do indeed? This was a question I had faced for one and a half years.

I couldn't believe that I hadn't seen or held Justin for such a long time. And yet I did somehow feel that he was with me in spirit. At night, I would ask him to give me a cuddle and tell him how much I loved him. In the mornings, the first thing I would say as I woke was, 'Good morning, *Mon Amour*, I love you so much … please tell me you are here.' I pulled myself together that day but, still, sadness shadowed me.

Rising at dawn one morning in the town of Kalpa some 3300 metres above sea level, I went outside to take in the view. It was crisp and cold, the sky a brilliant blue, with the outline of a row of snowy mountain peaks glimmering silvery-gold as the sun rose behind them. I felt I could reach out and touch with my hands the sacred mountain, Kinnaur Kailash, towering over 6000 metres high, even though it was kilometres away across the valley. Around me, the only sounds I could hear were the wind and the distant clank of a goatherd's bell.

Amid this peace and beauty, my throat suddenly felt like it was coated with glass. I felt my heart constricting and before I knew it, tears came rolling out. I felt so sad—and so alone. I longed for my darling to walk in the sunshine with me. I imagined myself giving him a long, loving kiss. Overcome with emotion, I felt that no one in the world but Justin could have made me feel better just then. And it was the first time, really, that I was finally admitting it.

Sri Lanka had helped enormously to transform my panic attacks of grief to something less physically wrenching. But I was left with an infinitely mournful feeling. At any moment of the day or night, I would find myself closing my eyes, hearing Justin's voice and reliving a moment, a turn of phrase, a touch—all the loving memories I had of him.

It was the mountains that did it. Mountains always brought me back to Justin. And now, high in the mountains and relating much more strongly to gentle, wise Kamal than my new German friends, a lot of memories were flooding back. I wasn't only thinking of Justin, I was remembering with pain and longing all the happy times I'd had with Deuchar, Nato and Paddy.

All that grief had changed me. Before Justin's death, I barely knew what fear was, but since then I had begun to fear horrible things happening all the time. One of my biggest fears was that something would happen to my sister Annie's kids, Tom, Charlie and Lucy. That thought would always freeze me in my tracks. I couldn't bear it; I felt like they were my own children. Then, suddenly, a realisation: if Justin had still been alive perhaps I would have been pregnant by now. Thoughts like these, which seemed out of my control, pierced my heart.

Over and over I would wrench myself back to reality and try and appreciate the astounding place I was in. Every day, we'd visit a different valley or a different town, driving for hours across rivers that frothed like chocolate milkshakes, our jeep occasionally gasping and belching in the high altitudes. There were checkpoints where uniformed officials would verify our permits and roadblocks caused by falling rocks or melted ice. We'd cross roads submerged in icy water as rivers overflowed with melting snow in the Indian Himalayan spring. I'd close my eyes, trying not to think how much and how often we were tempting fate.

At the intersection of the Sutlej and Spiti rivers, the terrain began to change and by the time we reached the village of Nako the architecture had morphed from wooden houses to brick dwellings. Roofs were made of prickle bush or straw and the terrain was transformed from field-like to rocky. The people's features were Tibetan; the lifestyle was Buddhist; sheep, goats and cows strolled about everywhere; prayer wheels dotted the streets as regularly as traffic lights in downtown Sydney. It was hard to believe we were still in India!

A lake formed the village centrepiece, surrounded by fields of peas and potatoes, immaculately fenced and terraced. Our little group climbed up higher to visit some of the gleaming white temples that were perched on the red-brown rock of the mountainsides with prayer flags flapping. We fell silent as we took in the spectacle. We watched the river turn brown, then blue, then silver in the setting sun and when it was over, I walked back alone, feeling the need for solace.

In the ferociously beautiful Spiti Valley, with its arid valley floor and mountain settlements carved into the side of foreboding cliff faces, we would stop occasionally to visit one of the myriad monasteries in the region. At the village of Laluna, a beautiful monk with a captivating aura invited Kamal and me inside to do some yoga stretches and partake of green tea after our class. I found myself calmed by the yoga and transfixed by the monk's beautiful, open face and his relaxed, easy gestures.

I could almost feel my heart open wider to meet the monk's openness and by the time Lama G (as he asked to be called) took Kamal and me on a tour of his lovingly tended 1004-year-old temple, I was beginning to tremble with feelings. The kindly monk showed us the temple's richly coloured, gold-leaf paintings depicting the various stages of Buddha's life and then began reading out loud in Tibetan some scripts recounting Buddha's teachings. His voice was calm and sonorous as Kamal and I listened. I found myself yet again in tears.

The longer and higher we trekked in the mountain kingdoms, the more I cried. By the time we reached Kaza, where we refuelled at what is proudly proclaimed to be the highest retail outlet in Asia, my wheels began to fall off. We'd been driving, hiking and sightseeing for days and everywhere I looked, there were mountains towering above and around me, piercing blue skies, beautiful, enchanting people who didn't seem to hold the capacity for judgement or criticism, and always the calming presence of our guide, Kamal. I felt blessed to be in such a magical world, but I also strongly felt … life isn't fair.

Once I allowed such self-pity to settle in my heart, a rush of melancholic thoughts were unleashed. As a little girl, I had always dreamed of getting married. I had never imagined, though, that I would meet someone who would love me as much as I would love him. I always thought, for some strange reason, that I would love more than I would be loved.

Melon told me once how happy she was when Justin and I fell in love. There were so many 'Libbies', she told me. There was the daggy boarding school Libby that she loved dearly; there was socialite Libby; there was staunch, strong and loyal friend Libby; there was the sporty, workaholic, push-herself-to-the-limit Libby; and there was the soft, gentle, peaceful Libby I had apparently been when I was with Justin. 'I've never seen two people so happy, I've never seen two people who complemented each other so well,' Melon told me.

Why did it have to end so quickly? I asked myself again and again. Had our love been too powerful? Was it not meant to endure? Then I'd think, no, Justin and I both deserved to enjoy what we found with each other. There were no lessons we needed to learn; there was no need for him or me to grow stronger. So why did this happen to me? I was a good person; did I really deserve this? Perhaps it wasn't about me? Around and around it went, pointless, painful and endless.

CHAPTER SEVEN
AN IGLOO IN THE JUNGLE

On Kamal's advice, our party of four continued heading northwards in the shadow of the Zanskar Range that divides India from Tibet. The Spiti people, who are Indian but tend to resemble their Tibetan neighbours rather than their countrymen on the lower plains, were among the last mountain people to cede their independence to the British.

We meandered through the landscape with its intricate rocky outcrops and stopped briefly at the village of Sangam. Here, in honour of an impending visit by the Dalai Lama, scores of workers were constructing a new monastery to complement the 520-year-old structure already in existence. We lunched at a wonderful *dhaba* (roadside tea stall) and watched the adorable children at play.

After lunch we drove on and much to my chagrin, I found myself brooding again about what might have been. I was longing for Justin and the children we spoke about having; every toddler I saw, I wanted to pick up and hug. I went straight to my room when we reached our accommodation and slept badly. By dinnertime I was struggling to keep my composure. When I got up to return to my room Kamal was not far behind, on the pretext of bringing me a blanket. He asked me what was wrong and I burst into a flood of tears and told him my story.

Kamal listened very carefully and told me how, when his mother had died, he had cried for three years until one day a young woman had spoken seriously with him.

She had told him that he was a sad man and that nothing good would be attracted to him until he showed inward and outward happiness. Kamal also told me that he would pray for me, and that he would never forget me.

I told Kamal about the gifts Justin had given me— solid roots for strength and stability, and wings to fly, in order to achieve whatever my heart's desire. Kamal again listened quietly, obviously moved. In turn, I was touched by his sensitivity. I felt as if my words fell on the softest, most yielding ears; that Kamal truly cared about my suffering and did not judge. My wise driver had said that if I continued to cry for all my loved ones that had died, all of my friends would be sad that I was so sad. It was time, Kamal suggested, for them to see me happy.

I sighed—easy to say, less straightforward to apply. I would have liked to exude happiness, but it took a lot of strength and energy now. Once upon a time, being happy had come naturally, now I had to work at it.

It was difficult for our group to decide each day which direction we should take next. The relentless sunshine was melting many of the surrounding snow-capped mountains, resulting in avalanches, landslides and rivers bursting their banks. Fording rivers high in the shadows of the peaks was a scary business. Sometimes a group of truck drivers would meet, consult and drive in convoy, allowing us to join them, thereby ensuring manpower and emergency help should a river wash a jeep downstream or a boulder the size of a house block a path.

Shortly after leaving Kaza we learned that a pass had completely disappeared after the side of a mountain slid away in a rockslide. It would take 14 days to re-open. The damage was so bad that the Chief Minister of India was supposedly coming to inspect it. My travelling companions were impatient to move on, but we weren't going anywhere fast. Instead, we had to set up an outdoor camp for the duration.

I was secretly pleased at this unexpected turn of events, as I always enjoyed cooking on my Trangia and liked nothing more than to sleep in my tent. I rustled up a little tomato and garlic pasta for the group and Kamal and I then sat huddled in the cold night air telling each other ghost stories and counting the falling stars. Just as I was launching into another story, Kamal asked me to pass the torch. He flashed the light at the brush behind us and very quietly instructed, 'Quickly, follow me to the jeep! There's a snow leopard out there'.

I only had to hear it once—I was in the jeep in a flash and determined to sleep there all night, if need be. I saw a pair of eyes shining in the darkness, and my skin went cold. We were extremely lucky to have come across one of these rare creatures, but was this a good time? Kamal pointed out that we were camped around a watering hole and our tents were full of food. The leopard was probably hungry and could smell our provisions. Kamal woke Det and Eve once we felt safer and made a fire to frighten away the animal.

The next day, Kamal and I went on a long hike, reaching 4100 metres with no signs of altitude sickness, and had a picnic in the ruins of a Tibetan Buddhist monastery, Gompa Hikkum. I chatted like a budgerigar, feeling very close to my new best friend with whom, by now, I had shared so much. Descending, I began to feel the effect of days of endless hiking over continually steep, rocky terrain. Bang, bang, bang went my toes against the inside of my boots until I thought my feet were going to explode. Again, Kamal showed nothing but patience and concern for my distress although, thankfully, it was only physical this time. I was losing some toenails, but I wasn't losing my perspective.

The next day, after tending my feet and enjoying a good night's sleep, we heard the good news that one of the passes had opened early and bolted into action. An arduous 12-hour drive ensued, during which we spotted several cyclists puffing their way up hills 4800 metres above sea level. I stared at them with envy and knew this was something that Justin and I would have done; people would have labelled us crazy, but we would have relished the challenge and competitively strained to keep each other going longer, higher, better.

Finally, our group made it to Kunzum Pass, surrounded by towering snow-covered mountains and monastery prayer flags flapping in the breeze. Magical!

After a short stop, we descended until we reached the town of Batal, a tented campsite where we ate the best dhal, peas and rice I've ever tasted. A nervous driver asked Kamal if he could ride with us in convoy and my admiration grew even further. Not only was Kamal the gentlest and kindest guide you could find, he also seemed to be revered by other locals as a master driver who knew the mountains intimately.

By the time we got to the larger town of Keylong and shared 'family room' accommodation with Det and Eve, I was in high spirits. The entire journey had been spectacular; the arid, rocky gorges we had traversed were a formidable, remote beauty.

In Keylong I met some other Westerners. It was particularly good to chat to Corinne, a mountain rescuer from Chamonix who hiked most European summers in the Himalayas. Her boyfriend, Christian, had climbed Everest and K2 without oxygen, written various mountaineering books and was head of several mountaineering associations in France. In a typically brief but intense encounter, we shared our views about life, death, philosophy and religion and promised to stay in touch. This is an aspect of travelling that I've always enjoyed; I've tended to follow up on chance encounters and typically found that a door to new experiences has been opened.

The following morning we all rose at 2.30 am for the long drive to Leh, cultural heart of the province of Ladakh, north of Himachal Pradesh, and hoped to cover most of the trickier terrain before the midday sun began its treacherous snow-melting work. But two hours later, we hit our first roadblock: a huge boulder in the middle of a river crossing with trucks and jeeps queued for miles on either side. Only a bulldozer would move a rock this big and help wouldn't come for hours, so we all settled down to sleep. Around 7 am, a few jeeps started to inch their way around the boulder and succeeded, so we decided to try as well. We edged slowly across the river with water reaching almost the top of our tyres and fought to hold on as we were thrown about in the humping, snarling vehicle. We somehow made it, but I had my eyes tightly shut the entire time.

About two hours later, another impasse, this time a jeep caught in a stream. It was freezing cold up here at 4800 metres above sea level but Kamal jumped out to help and within seconds was knee-deep in icy water trying to push the jeep out. It took 30 minutes and the strength of over a dozen men, but the near impossible was finally achieved. We were off again, four hours late and starting to worry about the impending Baralacha La Pass, where a bridge had been destroyed. We had to reach this pass, 4950 metres above sea level, before the waters rose too high.

By the time we got there, we were in a dreamland of blue, blue sky and lush white snow and ice. Silence descended on our jeep as we all took in the view, hushed and awed by the mystical snow-covered wonderland that enveloped us. In the midst of this magical terrain, we spied several army camps for soldiers en route to Kashmir where skirmishes on the India-Pakistan border continued.

We made it through the pass, had some food and set off again for Ladakh's capital, Leh, in a small, fertile valley north of the Indus River. After resting our travel-sore bottoms, we planned to spend some days exploring this former outpost on the ancient trading caravan route. We arrived close to midnight and struck travellers' gold   private rooms, a shower and comfy beds.

We awoke to an amazing contrast from the landscape we'd travelled in the previous day. Never before had I seen such a desolate place. In every direction the eye met only monotonously dreary rock and stone.

As it happened, the Dalai Lama himself was flying into the settlement the morning we arrived. Eve and I joined the throng of Buddhist pilgrims lining the road along which His Holiness was scheduled to drive en route to a nearby monastery. All the locals were dressed to the nines in their traditional garb of bright, embroidered winged hats and pointy-toed shoes, while each schoolchild waved the Tibetan Buddhist colours of yellow, green, red, white and blue, signifying earth, water, fire, cloud and sky. Countless pilgrims also carried floral tributes as offerings to Buddha's representative on earth.

But in the end, the much-anticipated appearance was more temporal than spiritual. The Dalai Lama's vehicle appeared only briefly and flashed past in a blink-and-miss-it moment.

Kamal and I headed off to stroll through Leh, talking at length about life and all the while trying new foods at local *dhabas*, shopping for souvenirs, and visiting Leh's pride and joy, its eco-centre. Formidable Swedish-born Helena Norberg-Hodge had settled in the area and planted willow and poplar trees, transforming this section of her dustbowl environs to something somewhat greener. Here too, Ladakh's populace tended to be environmentally savvy, conscientious especially about keeping their settlements plastic-free. Several excellent bakeries, offering the customer delicious freshly baked pumpernickel bread as well as tasty yak and goat's cheese, were further testament to the good woman's influence, while freshly squeezed buckberry juice and tasty dried apples and apricots were also available for sampling at the centre.

Further temptations in the form of many colourful bazaars also prompted me to loosen my purse strings. I bought two beautiful, intricately woven carpets, a couple of pashminas and browsed through the antiques and silver, coral and turquoise jewellery. Then we sat down to another meal of delicious Tibetan food. After many *dhaba* stops in the past weeks, and with Kamal as my trusty mentor, I had become a fan of the local cuisine, especially *parathas*, the local bread fried on an oil griddle, filled with vegetables and chilli, for breakfast. By this stage, I was also chowing down *momos* (a type of Tibetan steamed spring roll) and all manner of *thukpa*, *thantuk* and *chowtse pe* (soups with vegetables, dumplings, noodles or wontons) and thoroughly enjoying the experience. In the cold mountain air, such food seemed to restore one's natural sense of balance and harmony.

Our final destination as a group was Manali, in the fertile Kullu valley, roughly halfway between our northernmost point, Leh, and Shimla, where we had started. I was mindful that these were my last days with Kamal and already began to feel mild pangs of separation. The truth was, I had bonded far more with this local than I had with my Western travelling companions. I knew I would hold Kamal and his homeland—a magical realm of mountains, snow and intensely bright blue skies at the top of the world— forever in my heart.

Travelling downhill we met nomads camped along the plains and stopped to offer provisions. After distributing water and food, we visited their camping site. Looking at the nomads' primitive facilities—their total worldly possessions were their home-made tents and sleeping mats, yak fur coats and boots, yak dung for cooking over an open fire, a posse of crazy dogs and their herds of yak and goat—I felt awed by the stoicism these people needed to keep going. The hardships were plain enough to see in their grimy, wind-chapped faces, matted hair and rough, gnarled hands.

Later, as we pitched a tent for the night, Kamal and I played cricket—he bowled me out—and went for a long, bracing walk to build up an appetite and stretch our legs. While walking, we spotted an enormous wolf, my first ever sighting of such a beast, and I nearly jumped out of my skin. I was suprised again the following day as we headed southwards via Rohtang Pass to discover that the area was hopping with carnival festivity. On the one side of the pass a sleepy hamlet perched quietly on the mountainside, but around a hairpin bend it was a different matter altogether, as hundreds of buses transported revellers up the steep ascent to Rohtang's party site. After weeks in the peaceful, quiet surrounds of higher, drier, cooler and more sleepy Tibetan-influenced villages, my eyes popped when I spied the crowds.

Family members, young and old, queued up for hours to pay their fee for a yak, pony, tyre or toboggan ride and everywhere the air was filled with screeches of delight. There were skiing competitions for the more adventurous while others would scoot down the hill on a piece of cardboard or sacking, tumbling at the bottom with delighted whoops, and immediately returning to the queue for another go. Everywhere you looked, there were merchants touting hot corn, fairy floss and the obligatory roasted peanut snacks.

While locals meandered about the fairgrounds in the moderate above-zero temperatures, some visitors from the hot plains below were obviously struggling with the cooler mountain climes, and there was a booming business in thick fur coats and gumboots for hire. After enjoying the mayhem for a while, our group hit the road once more.

In Manali, after three weeks on the road together, it was time to say goodbye to Kamal. He gave me one of his favourite cassettes of Tibetan music and I gave him the equivalent of six months' local salary as a gift. One thing you realise in India is that every white visitor is a millionaire and that it is relatively easy to make a big difference, fiscally speaking, to one local's life.

By the time I reached McLeod Ganj, a nineteenth century British garrison town that gradually developed as a hill station to nearby Dharamasala, I was disorientated and tired. Having travelled solo on a bus for hours, I was in serious need of rest so, once my accommodation was sorted out, I booked myself in for a one and a half hour Tibetan massage and gave myself over to my masseur, Pini, who told me his colourful life story.

Like so many Tibetans, Pini had fled the arrival of the Communist Chinese in his home country, travelling on foot for 21 days to Nepal. The last four, he told me, were in snow, freezing, without food. When he finally reached a sanctuary, he was offered two choices: the life of a monk or a scholar. He chose schooling and studied for three years before setting up his own massage practice and ultimately settling in Dharamasala—a Tibetan refugee metropolis that was home to a quarter of a million people in similar circumstances, including the fourteenth Dalai Lama.

Unfortunately, too many travellers are drawn to this remote corner of the Indian Himalayas by the Dalai

Lama's reputation. While the attraction might be spiritual, the garish, overpopulated town is in stark contrast to the simple, unpolluted beauty of the villages in surrounding valleys. I felt no desire to tarry longer than necessary here, and within days had bought a ticket back to Delhi.

By the time I reached Anjula's flat in the hip suburb of Vasant Vihar, I noticed Delhi's scorching heat was now laced with unbelievable humidity. I went a few days later to a downtown Internet cafe and emailed some friends with news of my travels. As I typed, the roof thundered with monsoon rains and three cows appeared at my elbow, just outside the shop, contentedly adding their droppings to the layers underfoot. Amazing India. I was sorry to leave, but friends awaited me in nearby Nepal and my flight was booked.

A few days later, I was catapulted into the cooler, more serene world of Kathmandu and the initial omens were good. At the airport, I was whisked away by a driver to Jim Edwards's place, fondly known as The White House. Jim was an elephant polo friend (inventor of the sport with Manclark) and owner of Nepal's best-known luxury jungle retreat, Tiger Tops. Not for the first time, I silently blessed Geoffrey for making all these friendships possible.

This wasn't my first visit to the kingdom and it, too, had experienced tragedy in the period since I last visited. Two years earlier, the bloodiest, most complete massacre of any royal family in the modern age took place when Nepal's Crown Prince Dipendra slaughtered almost his entire immediate family (and then himself) in a volley of bullets within the palace walls.

As the fascinating book *Blood Against the Snows* explained it, it would have been akin in Britain to Prince Charles shooting dead Queen Elizabeth and Prince Philip, his brothers Edward and Andrew, Princess Anne, his own sons William and Harry and finally, himself, leaving only his aunt, Princess Margaret to assume the throne. And the motive? If you were to carry through the analogy, it would be because the House of Windsor, headed by the Queen, was united in its plans to stop Prince Charles marrying Camilla Parker Bowles.

In Crown Prince Dipendra's case, the woman at the heart of the furore was Devyani Rana, a beautiful, smart commoner from a wealthy industrialist family whom the royal family had deemed unsuitable for marriage. The bright, university-educated aristocrat fled Nepal for Europe after the massacre and has not been heard of since.

The bloodshed illustrated effectively how Nepal, even in the twenty-first century, remained shackled to a past where royal bloodlines are considered sacrosanct and more worthy of reverence than democracy. This came about partly because Nepal is the only country in the world that has never been occupied by foreign powers

nor been subjected to colonial rule, allowing the
kingdom to evolve at its own somewhat impoverished
pace, while also permitting misguided notions and
blinkered mind-sets to flourish. The Nepalese have
long suffered from tyranny as a result, but they have
had the satisfaction at least of knowing that it was at
the hands of their own. Times have changed, however,
and despite multi-party elections since 1991 the
country has remained plagued by corruption and
turmoil, compelling the King to repeatedly step in and
call for unity. When Crown Prince Dipendra effectively
brought to an end the Shah dynasty that had reigned in
Kathmandu since 1769, the kingdom's stability came
under additional threat.

For people like Jim Edwards, the outcome of the
massacre was inevitable: at any signal of instability,
tourists shy away and the situation was not helped by the
increased activity of power-hungry Maoists who took
advantage of the turmoil following the massacre. (King
Gyanendra, one of the dead King's younger brothers,
was installed as Nepal's new ruler. As his bloodline is
considered weaker, the general feeling appears to be that
his leadership is also weaker.) The upshot was that hotels
operated at a fraction of their capacity, traders' tills
stood empty and the local populace suffered more.

Tourists were few and far between, but I found myself
in luck after scouting around the capital for fellow
travellers willing to join me on the proposed next leg of
my travels: a pilgrimage in the remote western regions of

Tibet. A Brazilian-born stockbroker from New York and his French wife declared their interest and suggested we depart in ten days' time. I found myself, unexpectedly, in soothing surroundings with plenty of time to rest and relax.

And in no time at all, thanks to the Edwards's connection, I was swept up by the energies and exuberances of a colourful, sociable crowd that included Nepal's most talented (and Vienna-trained) architect, a glamorous French couple working for the Red Cross, various members of the British military and a number of overseas-educated Nepalese.

At the centre of this extraordinary clique was Kristjan Edwards, Jim's son, a charismatic professional polo player, former cresta champion and world class fly-fisherman, who smoked and drank up a storm as he cajoled all and sundry to live life to the full. Also attendant was Kristjan's girlfriend, Hattie, a long-legged vivacious blonde, and Kristjan's sister, Anna-Tara, visiting from the US. While Kristjan and Anna-Tara exchanged pleasantries in a language that I found impossible to identify, I was discreetly informed about the siblings' Icelandic roots and their melancholic mother who had died some years previously in a bath.

Possibly in tribute to their roots, 'ice' became the *mot du jour* and before we knew it, Kristjan was inviting us all to an 'ice party' in the Royal Chitwan National Park. With 300 workers laid off at Tiger Tops following the royal family scandal and the ensuing tourist drought, the blond-haired playboy suddenly found himself with relatively little to do. Much like his adopted country, Kristjan was struggling to find a way forward as the new millennium dawned. His stopgap solution, however, was straightforward—when in doubt, party. So before we knew it, a band of us were being primed for a four-day bash in the jungle during monsoon season. Kristjan went ahead with his architect friend Prabal to prepare, while Hattie, Anna-Tara and I followed by jeep, trailed by other vehicles crammed with party-goers.

We drove all morning in the rain until we reached a river and stopped for lunch. A film crew, arranged by Kristjan to document the entire proceedings for posterity, set to work as we clambered into a boat to cross the seething river and then climbed aboard a second jeep waiting for us on the riverbank. I'm not sure how he managed to organise all this transportation so quickly and efficiently but by the time Kristjan met us, astride an elephant and proffering ice-cold white wine, I was drenched from the jungle steam and full of anticipation.

It soon became apparent that we were all participants in a theatrical production masterminded by our host. We yielded to the moment and sure enough, Ice Extravaganza (as we dubbed it) was a head-spinning experience from the second we climbed aboard our elephants. With wineglasses in hand, and *mahouts* leading the charge, we proceeded to lumber through the rainforest to the lodge's front steps, where we were greeted by more hospitable *wallahs* (employees) in fine livery, brandishing further refreshments.

After a raucous night of fine food, lashings of alcohol and cosmopolitan conversation, I awoke late and headed straight for the kitchen to rustle up some salads to accompany the pig-on-the-spit planned for the night's festivities. As Hattie and I peeled, diced and chopped together, she confided all sorts of worries about the future of her relationship and that of Nepal, but I found it difficult in my festive mood to delve beyond the conviviality. Throwing off my apron after a couple of hours' work, I gave myself over to fun. With Nepali architect Prabal close on my heels, I swam across the rushing river, walked a few kilometres upstream and then threw myself into the frothing torrent, allowing myself to be swept downstream. Prabal and I did this over and over until we were close to dropping with exhaustion, and then returned to the lodge in time for a 'disco nap' before the big party.

Emerging later for cocktails, I was met by the most astounding sight. Directly in front of the lodge's open-air terrace, on a lush lawn amid dense jungle foliage, was a two and a half-metre high, three-metre wide igloo, miraculously erected out of giant blocks of ice that had been transported on trucks from ice factories kilometres away. Behind the igloo, the river flowed past in a soft torrential rush and beyond that, appearing from behind a bank of thick, fluffy rain clouds, were the jagged snow peaks of the Annapurna range. It was breathtaking. In fact, the whole night was unforgettable, beginning with chocolate and chilli vodkas and ending some 16 hours later when all that was left of the igloo was an enormous puddle.

After dinner, 50 Nepalese drummers made their appearance from a nearby camp, accompanying their instruments with deep, low chants to create a heartbeat that thumped like elephants moving through underbrush. People began to dance spontaneously on the lawn as the drummers formed a circle and before I knew it, I was among the gaggle, shimmying and swaying, grooving and gliding as I allowed the music to throb right through me. I could feel my control button switching off as I gave myself over to the moment. Prabal, rapidly becoming my new best friend, jumped up to join me and we urged each other on, moving in rhythm to the clapping, throbbing, chanting pulses of the jungle beat.

After 15 minutes of this feverish trance, we made a dash for the igloo and threw ourselves onto the fellow revellers who were already inside cooling off. Once inside, the igloo dripped all over us and we began to freeze. That was Kristjan's Icelandic inspiration—you know, hot geyser baths, then a dip in freezing cold water, all supposedly excellent for circulation. We laughed uproariously as we cooled off and then threw ourselves right back into the fray.

A local Nepali grabbed my hand, led me to the clearing in front of the drummers and invited me to join him. Prabal, shimmying and shaking himself, beamed conspiratorially as I threw my arms up in the air and launched myself with gusto into the spirit of the occasion. Before I knew it I was performing the dance of the wild boar (up on my 'hinds'), the dance of the elephant (flat on my belly), and various suggestive fertility dances. I felt sufficiently lubricated to let go of all my inhibitions and noticed many of my newfound friends and fellow guests felt the same way. My dance partner was thrusting his pelvis suggestively, his tongue hanging out and his eyes agog, and I found myself stifling a giggle, unable to return his attentions. Others were egging us on, hopeful, I sensed, that I would fall into my partner's arms.

Thankfully, Hattie suddenly appeared. 'Come, Kristjan needs us,' she announced in an urgent whisper as she guided me away. I was grateful to escape my dance partner's clutches, but Hattie was not being philanthropic. Kristjan did need us. Our genial host had surpassed himself with the staging of his jungle fiesta but had imbibed, like many of his guests, one thirst-quenching drink too many and was beginning to suffer the consequences. Hattie and I found him sprawled in front of his precious igloo, his glass draining across the grass with a soft fizz.

I looked around at the festive gathering and saw our host wasn't the only one who had drunk one too many chilli vodkas. I smiled to myself. Our maestro might not remember too much about his crazy jungle fiesta, but I knew this was one party I wouldn't forget.

All my troubles and sorrows were swept away that weekend. For the first time in a long time I believed again that I was the sort of woman who would jump first into a river on a dare, who could climb back on a horse after a fall, and who would happily dance, carefree, on tables when the music called. There in the jungle, I rediscovered the woman I'd been before my heartbreak.

I vividly remember the thought coming to me like a cool breeze as I danced and danced and danced that night—perhaps I could be happy again.

CHAPTER EIGHT
A SACRED PILGRIMAGE

Back very briefly in Kathmandu, Prabal took me out for pizza and despite our mutual exhaustion after endless partying and interminable travelling, we still managed to talk and flirt. As we kissed on the lips briefly at the end of the night, my heart missed a beat, but I tried not to react. It was midnight and a taxi was picking me up at 5 am to meet my new travelling companions on my long-yearned-for journey to Tibet.

The following morning, after little sleep, I felt excitement about the next leg of my travels. With Brazilian-born stockbroker Felipe and his French-speaking artist wife, Elizabeth, I was headed for the western region of Tibet known as Ngari to see for myself 'the navel of the world', the source of Asia's four greatest rivers, sacred Mt Kailash.

I remember clearly how captivated I was the first time I read in the inspiring book *Tibet: Relflections from the Wheel of Life* about Mt Kailash—a great black rock soaring to 6714 metres, with the distinction of being the world's most venerated holy place and also the least visited because of its remote location. 'No planes, trains or buses travel anywhere near the region,' I read, 'and even with rugged overland vehicles the journey still requires weeks of difficult, often dangerous travel.'

After visiting the Indian Himalayas and meeting various Buddhists in Kathmandu, I became even more determined to visit, attracted to the mountain's remoteness and the adventure implicit in the rugged pilgrimage. Also, the holy mountain was in Tibet. Here, in one of the poorest countries in the world, people practise 'being happy' the way Westerners strive for success, whatever that is. Buddhism was a philosophy that appealed to me far more than the religion I imbibed from childhood, which seemed to me based on fear, retribution and an endless litany of rules and regulations.

I was headed to Mt Kailash for inspiration. Situated in one of the most desolate and inaccessible corners of the globe, the mountain Tibetans call Ghang Rimpoche or 'precious jewel of snows' has long been an object of worship. The ancient Tibetan Bön people revere the mountain, as do the followers of the Jain religion, while for the Buddhist faithful, this mountain is the abode of Demchok, a fierce manifestation of Buddha.

The book went on to explain that Hindus, meanwhile, believe Mt Kailash to be the abode of Lord Shiva and that 'according to legend, immortal Shiva lives atop Kailash where he spends his time practising yogic austerities, making joyous love with his divine consort, Parvati, and smoking ganja, the sacred herb known in the west as marijuana … For a Hindu, to make the arduous pilgrimage to Kailash and have the *darshan* (divine view) of Shiva's abode is to attain release from the clutches of ignorance and delusion …

Pilgrims to Kailash, after the difficult journey getting there, are then confronted with the equally arduous task of circumambulating the sacred peak.' Walking around the mountain is known as a *kora* and normally takes three days but I was amazed to discover that 'in hopes of gaining extra merit or psychic powers, some pilgrims will vary the tempo of their movement. A hardy few, practising a secret breathing technique, will power themselves around the mountain in only one day. Others will take up to three weeks by making full body prostrations the entire way.

Most pilgrims to Kailash will also take a short plunge in the nearby, highly sacred (and very cold) Lake Manasarovar; the name meaning "lake of consciousness and enlightenment". This kind of pilgrimage is considered not only a life-changing experience, but also an opportunity to view some of the most magical scenery on the entire planet.' I was full of anticipation.

The Chinese government doesn't make it easy, however, for Westerners travelling solo to join pilgrims in their quest. To complete the fabled pilgrimage, a Westerner is compelled to hire the services of a government-approved guide and driver and make up a group with at least two others—hence, the need to hook up with Felipe and Elizabeth. Getting the paperwork approved is another hurdle: as the three of us eyed each other up somewhat uneasily that morning, mindful that we would be experiencing unknown territory together, I silently prayed Mt Kailash would provide me with some answers.

Thankfully, a long drive through the lush Nepalese foothills stretched ahead. With the Himalayas providing a reassuring backdrop and the Friendship Bridge at the Nepalese–Tibetan border at least a six-hour drive away, I decided to leave small talk with my fellow travellers for another day. I zoned out, content to simply loll along in my fiesta-induced stupor.

As we drove, the scenery became more spectacular, but my condition deteriorated. Lack of sleep after days of carousing had given rise to flu-like symptoms, including sore glands and a body that ached all over. All malaise was temporarily forgotten, however, as we crossed the Nepalese–Tibetan border at Kodari, only recently reopened after a SARS virus scare. It was crazily chaotic with not a Westerner in sight, just crowds of Indian pilgrims. We filled out departure forms and I remembered in the nick of time that I had dozens of photographs with me of the Dalai Lama. I knew that Chinese officials would confiscate them summarily— any form of recognition of Tibet's spiritual leader was strictly verboten—so I hurriedly entrusted my collection to a guide returning to Kathmandu.

One Brazilian *homem*, a French *demoiselle* and one Aussie sheila—the sum total of our Western coterie gingerly made our way across the Friendship Bridge to the Chinese border post where a long queue awaited us. Our guide, speaking in bite-sized English, hurried over and introduced himself as Jampa. He got to work, immediately impressing us by getting us to the front of the queue. When the electronic thermometer was produced to take our temperatures (SARS fears), my heart fluttered in case these unfriendly looking officials were about to turf me out abruptly or quarantine me for days.

But all went well and after our passports were checked we trekked to our four-wheel drive, weaving uphill on foot behind Jampa, through throngs of black market moneychangers. Our driver, Tenzin, a friendly looking Tibetan who couldn't speak a word of English, awaited us at the vehicle, ready to set out on our journey. We drove uphill for another two kilometres and stopped again to present our passports, this time to immigration officials. I was first in line and seemed to throw the bureaucrats into a frenzy: tiny, white-faced men spoke rapidly to one another, gesticulating exuberantly and becoming quite agitated. It turned out that, as we hadn't handed over our group visa, they thought I was trying to travel alone and this of course was a big no-no.

We were then introduced to yet another Chinese edict when Jampa instructed us to turn our watches forward two hours. Even though we lay 4000 kilometres southwest of the Chinese capital, it was government regulation that locals operate according to Beijing time. This meant we were supposed to rise before the sun and fall to bed while the sun still shone. That's Chinese officialdom for you.

Formalities dealt with, we sat down to a lunch of fried rice before driving in heavy rain through a mossy gorge to our first port of call, passing torrential waterfalls on our way. Some cascaded down the mountainsides directly on to our moving vehicle, drenching us. It was frightening, yet exciting, and partly explained why our destination town, Nyalam, translates as 'gateway to hell' in Tibetan.

As our jeep climbed above the haze and approached Nyalam it rapidly became obvious that we were in a distinctly new country—*Tashi dele* Tibet! (hello Tibet!)

Now notices were almost exclusively in Chinese or Tibetan, with English a rarity except for an infrequent sign for a hotel or restaurant. Shops were filled with China's distinctively kitsch-cute packaged goods, while the local citizens appeared more sharply featured than the broader, more softly contoured Nepalese. Also, as one would expect after decades of communist rule, villagers were typically dressed in very plain pants and shirts that succeeded in making everyone blend into a sea of uniformity.

At our hostel in Nyalam we negotiated our rooms to about $AU3.50 a night. The beds seemed surprisingly comfortable, but the bathroom situation was vile. Then a convoy of Indian pilgrims arrived, about a dozen per jeep, and the hubbub never abated. I was so tired that I fell asleep despite their goings-on and found it hard to rouse myself to meet with our guide for dinner. As we sat there in the district's finest eatery, I realised that eating out was unlikely to restore my strength. On the contrary, the local cuisine might be good for weight loss. All the dishes seemed to be drenched in oil and MSG, making my lips numb and my chest feel like a brick was weighing it down.

I managed only a few spoonfuls of dinner and longed again for bed. Felipe and Elizabeth said very little as, like me, they tried to adjust to what we all three realised was going to be 28 long, hard days, even for experienced travellers. Back at the hotel, the three of us collided with more throngs of Indian pilgrims, but even so I fell asleep again surrounded by their cacophony.

The next morning, my head felt worse than ever. Kathmandu is at an elevation of 1300 metres, Kodari at 1873 metres. Nyalam, at 3750 metres above sea level, is almost 2000 metres higher again (for the record, Mt Everest is a sky-piercing 8848 metres). My *Lonely Planet* travel guide had specifically warned of altitude sickness in the early part of the Tibetan journey and here I was, weak and wobbly as we began the ascent through the country's higher plains. My head felt like it was clamped in a vice and being gradually screwed ever tighter, painfully reminding me of those months after Justin died when my days were filled with tears, depression, panic attacks and throbbing migraines. I couldn't begin to imagine the degree of fitness and acclimatisation we would need to climb to greater heights. After years of trekking, I had thought I was pretty fit, but as I nursed a throbbing head, I began to wonder.

Despite taking painkillers for my headache, my head continued to throb like a lama's gong. Breakfast didn't help either: a plain thick pancake with pineapple jam was all that was going. I longed for fresh fruit and vegetables, but they didn't seem to know such luxuries in China's Tibet. Carrots, cabbage and potatoes were the extent of it, not to mention the dreaded daikon radish, a sort of white cucumber that repeats on you if you nibble on it like a carrot, as I had. I finally learned my lesson and avoided this local delicacy.

The surroundings weren't helping either. So far, this was not the Tibet I had dreamt of! Everywhere I looked in Nyalam, ugly concrete high-rise blocks, heavily dependent on white lavatory tiles for architectural effect, overshadowed the few remaining rustic village dwellings. Streets were almost totally submerged under mountains of beer bottles, many of them broken. And everywhere, bureaucracy reigned, with impassive officers operating boom gates and checkpoints at alarmingly frequent intervals, demanding identification papers and travel visas with more than a hint of intimidation. On top of all this, rain drizzled down incessantly as we meandered through the muggy, hazy streets. So much for beautiful Tibet. During my first week, I just wanted to get the hell out.

Thankfully, Tenzin suggested a diversion. We drove ten kilometres north of the town to Milarepa's Cave. Milarepa was a famous Buddhist mystic who lived in the late eleventh and early twelfth centuries. As my *Lonely Planet* guide noted 'during a long meditation in his cave he apparently renounced all luxuries and survived on a diet of local weeds, (famously turning green as a result). He is credited with many magical feats in Tibetan literature; one was raising the ceiling of his cave with his bare hands.' Here, nestled in a beautiful valley of fluoro green barley and bright yellow canola, all sprinkled and intermingled with colourful wild flowers, Felipe, Elizabeth and I saw for ourselves, still visible on the cave's roof, the marks said to be the Tibetan saint's handprints.

After looking around the cave and the small temple built above it, my companions wandered off together outdoors, Elizabeth entranced by the sights and Felipe trailing in her wake. Throughout our trip, no matter how magical the sights, the Brazilian banker never stopped looking like he was out of his depth. I guessed this trip was his wife's dream, not his, and I admired him for tagging along.

For my part, I was happy to be rugged up in the coolish weather, wandering at last in a picturesque landscape. Strolling along the valley floor imbibing the hues and smells, I met a woman bent over with arthritis and we bowed deferentially to one another. I wondered what kind of life had rendered the old woman so crippled and who knows what she made of me, pale-faced and frizzy-haired, in my grey thermals and thick red fleece. Very briefly, our worlds collided.

The following morning we awoke early. Our fellow guests were out of control, but we were becoming accustomed to the ongoing mayhem. These pilgrims vomited, urinated, defecated and dumped rubbish with complete lack of restraint whenever and wherever they felt like it.

To escape our dirty, noisy 'base camp', Felipe, Elizabeth and I embarked on a seven-hour hike in the direction of a lake 4500 metres above sea level. Despite slathering on sunscreen, we burned as we walked in the thin air and sharp sun. Although I was in better shape than either Felipe or Elizabeth I was not as fit, alas, as I had hoped. I found myself huffing and puffing as we climbed, always thankful to collapse on a rock and eat my crackers and cheese, drinking in the views and vistas. The lake was worth the effort; the water glistened photogenically in the sunlight, encircled by wild flowers. We were all delighted to be here.

Whenever I was happy in nature, I found myself conjuring joyous memories of time spent with Justin. Whether we were skiing, sailing, hiking or mountain climbing, our adventures and dreams had been so well matched. We had both loved the outdoors. We felt inspired in nature and had recognised in one another a fellow mountain heart.

Awesome mountains notwithstanding, dust was everywhere in Tibet—in your jeep, in your backpack, in your clothes, in your sandwiches, between your toes, inside your ears, up your you-can-imagine-what. The sandy, desolate stretches of western Tibet, mystical lagoons and sacred mountains are not for those who can't get along without their creature comforts. In this neck of the woods a bath was more precious than gold, so when Felipe, Elizabeth and I discovered we could visit a Government-run bathhouse and enjoy a long hot shower, we were over the moon. Exhilarating views had nourished our souls, now our bodies were about to be pampered and we were delirious at the prospect. We relished the hot water and thorough scrubbing, knowing in advance that we'd have to wait at least a week to shower again.

After another bowl of greasy fried rice and another shared room with Felipe and Elizabeth, I went to bed. It pained me occasionally in their company to be reminded that I was alone, but I was also thankful that they were there when intruders would gaily walk into our lock-free room whenever they felt like it. The floorboards of our 'suite' were creaky, the beds lumpy and the prickly horsehair blankets and smelly rugs unable to completely insulate us from the cold, but at least I had company after a day outdoors that had lifted all of our spirits.

Sleep eluded all three of us, however, as drunken Tibetans painted the town red, Indian pilgrims shrieked through the night and road works commenced before dawn, making our beds, bedside tables and teacups rattle. At sunrise the next morning we finally, and joyously, departed a muddy Nyalam for Saga, nine hours away by car via Lalung La (an alarmingly lofty mountain pass at 5124 metres). Because it was cloudy, we could not see the mountaintops, but we spied various nomads with their herds of sheep and, in the passing fields, marmots, deer, domestic yaks and armies of field mice.

To reach Saga, a ferry ride was obligatory and we were downhearted to discover the ferry carried only two cars at a time. We got lucky however, driving aboard almost instantly. The other car on our trip had been waiting in convoy with 130 jeeps for six hours! There were no other European tourists around—the border having only recently been reopened after a long closure. I pinched myself with the realisation that I was truly, finally carrying out my sacred pilgrimage and that my dream of visiting Tibet was a reality.

The landscape was always surprising. One minute our jeep would be burrowing through a massive canyon, and then in no time at all we'd be traversing desert, then slicing through savannah or gliding along beside an aquamarine lake. Tibet's natural scenery was breathtaking, but the human elements were often appalling. Buildings looked like toilet blocks while toilet blocks were nothing more than squats; and everywhere, like a bad smell, was the presence of the military. Also, the further west we travelled in our quest to reach Mt Kailash, the more primitive and basic facilities became. Could the food get any worse, I wondered, or the accommodation? I shuddered and tried not to think too much about what lay ahead. The words of my Buddhist readings came back to haunt me: 'It is believed by the pilgrims that the greater the suffering, the greater the merit gained'. Could this be what they meant?

Dinner that night with Jampa and Tenzin in Saga's premier restaurant proved a treat with dishes served up by a sweet Chinese couple who had moved to western Tibet, encouraged by incentives offered by the Chinese government, in order to make a better life for themselves. I felt treacherous as I wolfed down my first appetising meal in over a week, knowing this kind of migration had made the Tibetan locals second-class citizens in their own country.

Getting fuel in Tibet was another slippery matter and certainly not as simple as driving to a petrol station and filling up. The trick was knowing fuel depot contacts and having sway with the local representatives. Tenzin, ever resourceful, tended to negotiate his way skilfully around these supply pitfalls so that we could always travel onwards. Before you could say 'fuel shortage', we'd be off again on a magical drive across green plateaus with snow-capped mountains in the background. Nomads in traditional clothing on horses draped in beautiful rugs galloped next to our jeep and we waved to one another.

I've always enjoyed car trips. Justin and I went, just the two of us, on a number of long ones in the first few months of our relationship and usually these involved a lot of sing-a-longs. So I felt right at home sitting in front with the always-cheery Tenzin who loved to sing along to his Tibetan tapes. The mood was festive and we all settled in for a long, lovely drive.

In Tibet, the hills were alive with music too, mainly the whistle of winds and the tinny sound of prayer wheels being turned as we passed monasteries and chanting monks. Spinning spindles creaked like rusty swings as they dispersed peace and harmony into the ether while somewhere in the distance, as we stopped to visit a shrine decorated with yak horns, another pack of rabid dogs would bark.

That evening at sunset, I sat on the front steps of a homely guesthouse on the outskirts of Paryang and scribbled in my diary surrounded by children, each one of them mesmerised by my pen as it moved over the paper. They were so fascinated by it that I felt compelled to hand over the pen, and the children squealed with delight. It was so easy, I found, to delight the local kids.

That night, Elizabeth and I strolled around Paryang, a dirt-poor village the size of two football fields with piles of rubbish on the sides of the road. It was dead flat, dusty, cold and about as inviting as another bowl of MSG. We pondered how people could live in such relentless desolation when we spotted, to our surprise, a sudden burst of lurid, living colour: a young girl in hot pink, fluoro red, green and blue costume was playing in a courtyard next to two men skinning a yak. Her playmate, in cool contrast, was dressed Westerner-style with a Nike cap worn backwards. Even here, in this isolated part of the world, the logos and slogans of multinationals were making their impact. Elizabeth and I looked around furtively and wondered what we'd see next—someone on a mobile phone perhaps?

Tenzin and Jampa sourced more fuel and we realised we were inching closer to our ultimate destination. Tenzin was delightful company, his lack of English notwithstanding, but our government-approved guide was another matter. Apart from his laziness and his inability to tell us much about the geographical highlights of the region (*Lonely Planet* was much more informative), Jampa would spend most of his time chewing on raw chicken's feet and spitting out crunchy claws and bones willy-nilly—not one of the most inspiring sights!

Finally, we arrived at the village of Hor Qu on the shores of holy Lake Manasarovar. We checked into a hostel with no toilet at all and frankly, that was a relief. We just wandered off into the wilderness, toiletries in hand, and hoped we didn't bump into anyone until the mission was accomplished!

The next day we rose at 5.30 am to begin the *kora* or holy circuit. Daylight peeped through just before 8 am, so we reached the gateway village of Darchen at the beginning of the trail just in time to watch a splendid sunrise. The sight of hundreds of pilgrims in the foreground performing their ablutions *au naturel* only marginally marred the experience. By now, our journey had become distilled to these fundamental activities: eating, sleeping, hiking and passing waste. For anything more, I realised, we would have to look inwards.

Before our pilgrimage to Mt Kailash began in earnest, we had to arrange two porters to help us carry our load, as we would be walking at altitudes up to 5600 metres above sea level. Just putting one foot in front of the other, let alone carrying provisions and gear, would be an achievement for anyone unaccustomed to such rarefied heights.

Solemnly, Tenzin, who would be waiting for us in Darchen, presented me with a plastic bag full of his baby's hair to place on the top of the Drölma La mountain pass, the highest point of the route we were about to walk counter-clockwise. I placed his offering carefully in my pocket, dreading the thought of losing his gift to the gods.

By 9.30 am we were ready to begin the 52-kilometre-long circuit and, as if on cue, the clouds lifted and the sacred mountain came into view, beckoning us. I should have been delirious to be finally fulfilling a long-held desire, but instead I felt overwhelmed by desolation. I had come here to bury my pain, but knots of sorrow still lay trapped within me. I unpacked my prayer flags, placed a few on a ribbon-festooned cairn and allowed myself to revisit the past. This was precisely what pilgrims were supposed to do at the outset of their journey. The first day was for remembrance of the past, the second day was for the death of the old self; and the third day, a rebirth, or renewal.

Before I knew it, tears were running down my cheeks unchecked as my thoughts turned to Justin. As I cried, I looked back on a full, exciting life that had felt as though it reached a pinnacle when Justin and I had admitted our love for one another. Some people never meet 'the right person' in their entire life and I had been lucky enough to fall in love with a man I respected on all levels. And then, all too soon, that perfect happiness had been taken away. As I pondered my life, I was reminded of Buddhism's four 'Noble Truths'.

The first of these: life is suffering. This suffering includes the loss of things we are attached to, and failure to achieve the things we desire. The second Noble Truth is that suffering lies in our desire for things to be other than what they are. This dissatisfaction leads us to react and these reactions typically lead to even more suffering. The third Noble Truth is that the cessation of desire brings an end to suffering. And the fourth Noble Truth says that when one ceases even to desire the cessation of desire, then one achieves nirvana, also known as 'beyond sorrow'.

Taking these philosophies to heart as a useful way to overcome despair, I took a deep breath and wiped away my tears, willing myself to find the courage and commitment to continue, simply, putting one foot in front of the other. I remembered the words of Justin who once told me in that thoughtful, kind way of his that 'dreadful things happen all the time. You mustn't allow it to shake your confidence in the world, because the world is still the same place. You are just beginning to understand it better'.

Warmed by the memory of these words, I continued to walk the circuit—Tibetan and Indian pilgrims occasionally overtaking me, but still looking almost as daunted by the climb as Felipe, Elizabeth and I.

We also occasionally saw pilgrims face down on the ground, making their way prostrate, which is the most powerful way of showing devotion. They had small wooden paddles attached to their hands for protection as they knelt; lay down; stood up; stepped forward; knelt; lay horizontal with their arms stretched out, and so on. Some pilgrims, I learned, do this circuit three, 13 or 108 times as a means of accumulating merit (*sonam*) or good luck (*tashi*). For me just doing it once was enough.

By the time we reached a river crossing almost seven hours later, Felipe, Elizabeth and I agreed we'd had enough for one day. I glugged down almost a litre of water with some gastrolytes, devoured a chocolate bar and slowly recovered some strength to set up my tent for an overnight stay, silently thrilled at the thought of sleeping alone in my very own space under the stars. I chose the perfect spot to pitch my tent: close to the river, out of the wind, with a beautiful view of the mountain. All I wanted now was Justin to share the moment with me …

Then, it all went awry. When I unpacked my equipment I realised my tent poles were missing. I had brought this tent with me all this way … for nothing! Disappointment, frustration, anger—I couldn't believe how close I was to a having a tantrum. Instead, I made my way to the monastery to join Felipe and Elizabeth for the night and when Elizabeth saw my face and asked what was wrong, I simply burst into tears and could not stop. As I cried, I noticed I had a large audience: roughly

50 workers left off their construction of a new wing for the monastery, while the temple lama also watched me, perplexed, surrounded by a small band of monks who stared with keen but silent curiosity.

Frankly, I didn't care; I couldn't stop crying. Thoughts kept swirling around in my head. I couldn't stop thinking about death, Justin, this world and my place in it, why this had happened to me, how I would go forward, Paddy and Nato. Death, too many deaths; how I wanted the pain to stop, how much I yearned to love and be loved again ...

I seemed to be falling apart—almost anything could reduce me to tears. Is this, I wondered, what a holy pilgrimage did to you? Did it break you down before it built you up again? I was too shattered, tired and confused to be sure any more of where my strong, confident self had gone.

My head was throbbing. Then the lama (whose title translates from the Tibetan as 'the unsurpassed') invited me into his chambers for tea. I followed his monks obediently, still sniffing, and they sat and stared at me. We had no common language, but it became obvious the lama wanted to know why I was crying. For the next half hour, we played charades as I explained my story. No, I was not crying because I didn't have tent poles; it was more complicated than that. I had lost the man I loved; I had lost the life together that we had planned. I had also lost so many dear friends, including some of the most important friendships in my life.

The lama listened and insisted that I keep chewing on the roasted barley flour dough, or *tsampa*, his monks proffered. He indicated that it would be good for my heart. He then bade the monks to leave and signalled for me to draw closer. Taking my hands in his, he butted his forehead against mine and began to mutter incantations I did not understand. He moved his head on either side of my head and kissed my temples and gestured for me to sit down again, all the while insisting I chew the unpleasant-tasting *tsampa*. Between that and the salty yak butter tea, I felt close to retching, but I also sensed that something important was afoot. The lama was intent on healing my sorrow.

He asked me to sit before him and when I obeyed, he put his hands on my heart and stomach and began praying, concluding with several blessings. Finally, looking into my eyes with a gaze that penetrated me to my core, he signalled that it was time for me to sleep. I was exhausted and, still weeping silently, I did as instructed and lay my sleeping bag on the dirt floor and closed my eyes.

Ten minutes later, I felt the lama shuffling through my blankets and lifting the arm that rested on my chest. I felt him put something in my hand and when I opened my eyes, saw it was a tiny, glistening crystal, cylindrical in shape, about the size of a tooth.

Holding the pale pink crystal in my fist close to my heart I closed my eyes again, listening as the lama and the monks chanted, prayed and beat their drums in the adjoining room. Finally, surprisingly gently, the noises subsided and I eased into sleep, the crystal seeming to exude curative powers as I sleepily remembered a dinner party in Delhi where a woman had told me I would meet a wise man on my travels 'who will look after you'.

For the next two days, as we waited for the weather to clear and our altitude headaches to subside, Lama Tsongkhapa and his trio of monks continued to feed, nurse, pray for and perform their therapy on me. And something miraculous happened in that dismal monastery in that desolate landscape: my sorrow was transformed to hope, joy and excitement about the future.

Up until the point I met Lama Tsongkhapa, it was as if all the grief and pain of the world was buried in my blood, skin and bones and this pain intensified when I first arrived. I felt 18 months of grief overwhelm me.

I became so drained by my suffering that I surrendered totally to Lama Tsongkhapa, desperate, I guess, for someone like him to help me. His prayers and ministrations were yet another precious gift. Thanks to him and his monks, I felt a gradual shift in my body as I convalesced on the outskirts of Mt Kailash. Like water draining from a pond, the pain began to seep away and I could sense buoyancy rather than lead in my heart.

It was as if the mountain and the lama drew out every
ounce of grief inside me and replaced it with lightness.
The lightness was not just physical, but mental too. Over
time, I found I had the inclination to do simple things
like read a book, which I had found hard to do since
Justin's death, and I discovered space in my head to
think about happy things. Until now, I had not been
able to think of the future in a positive light, but
on the second morning after another day of Lama
Tsongkhapa's ministrations, I remember thinking how
happy I was; how amazing my life was; and feeling
blessed that I had suffered as much as I had at such a
young age.

I sensed a strength and independence I hadn't sensed
before. I felt like my foundations had been rebuilt; that
I would manage whatever I came across in life. My
mind was clear and I was able to reflect on it all in a
truly positive way. I knew I still had an enormous
amount to learn, but I also knew that I had learned an
enormous amount. And I knew that the learning would
never stop.

Unmistakable stirrings of confidence began to flutter
in my chest and I realised I wanted to stand on my own
two feet emotionally. For so long, I had leaned on the
idea of Justin for emotional support and looked to him
to give me faith and answers. But now I felt assured: my
foundations were solid and I was ready to fly. I had not
yet circumnavigated Mt Kailash and already I was
beginning to feel reborn.

After 48 powerful hours, we farewelled Lama Tsongkhapa and his monks and set out again early, knowing we had another long hike ahead of us, carrying Tenzin's locket of hair with us to the heights of Drölma La at 5630 metres.

When I reached the pass, exhausted after a steep but exhilarating four-hour climb, I sat and looked all around me. The holy mountain was on my left, just an arm's distance away, and below glistened a turquoise lake speckled with white snow. The sky was bright blue, the odd cumulus cloud whisking through and showering us with the lightest of condensation. I sat, whispering the sentiments of Milarepa, the Buddhist yogi: 'There is no place more blessed or more marvellous than this'.

Within minutes, some pilgrims came and sat beside me. I pulled out my incense and handed some around, lighting it as we had a moment of Buddhist prayer. 'Omani padme om, omani padme om …'

I noticed how the Tibetan pilgrims were dressed: flip-flops, light woollen robes, no food or water. Temperatures were dropping and I was clad in beanie, gloves, fleece and Gortex jacket. All of our spirits were flying high. I didn't want to move and I didn't want my fellow pilgrims to go. Their presence felt so strong and so right. I had thought I would want to be alone at a moment like this, but instead I felt blessed to have fellow pilgrims around me. I felt privileged that they were including me in their celebrations.

Mt Kailash, I reflected, had not disappointed. As far as personal journeys went, this was better than I had ever imagined. The harsh climate and terrain and the exacting, exhausting conditions had tested me physically and emotionally and during this intense time, I had become weaker than I had thought possible—and grown stronger than I had ever been.

Ah Tibet! If I was disheartened at all, it was to have witnessed the influence of the Chinese in Tibet. I still feel angry today when I think about what the Chinese are doing to the country and its people. The Tibetan people have absolutely nothing. They are some of the poorest people I have ever seen. Their land is unbelievably dry and they're lucky as a result to grow any crops at all. Their culture and language have been torn away from them. They aren't even allowed to carry around a picture of their religious leader for fear of death or torture.

Not surprising then, that Tibetans look to something beyond their immediate surroundings for solace. Practically the only thing the Tibetan people have left—namely, a deeply held belief in the inherent joy of life—is, I believe, what ultimately keeps them going. It makes me sad that such a beautiful region with such beautiful people is gradually being destroyed.

As I contemplated the beauty and suffering of Tibet, I walked a short distance to find a place on the pass to erect my prayer flags for Justin. I had chosen the *Lung-ta* (Wind Horse) prayer flags, representing life's most uplifting energies. The Wind Horse is a mythical Tibetan creature from pre-Buddhist times that combines the speed of the wind and the strength of the horse to carry prayers from earth to the heavens. I was happy to imagine my prayers being carried by the wind to Justin; and I imagined him smiling when he noticed the renewed energy in my messages to him.

With every passing day, it was clearer that I felt differently about my losses. I no longer wanted to grieve and seek solace. Rather, I wanted to throw off my load and climb out of the bog of depression. I wanted to fly, scattering the last vestiges of my sorrow as I soared towards my future. It was time, I sensed, to finally let go. I was ready to engage in life again, and I looked forward to what lay ahead.

This sense of contentment continued to flourish as our group rested after our *kora* on the shores of magical Lake Manasarovar. I lay by the lake, closed my eyes and felt the sun's positive energy warm my bones. Occasionally, I would pull out my precious pink crystal from my jacket's inside pocket and watch it glisten in the sunlight. Destiny! I was meant to come here, I smiled to myself, and I was meant to be healed.

Later, when we walked out of the valley and returned to the gateway town of Darchen, where we were welcomed by a beautiful green, raging river and sunshine, we all expressed enormous relief to have completed the circuit. It had taken us four days rather than the usual three, but we had done it. I tied the last of my prayer flags to a rock and prayed to Shiva that henceforth, I would accept my sufferings. I'm not sure that Felipe and Elizabeth felt reborn, but I felt that I had jettisoned giant boulders of grief and was ready to face my future.

'*Mon Amour*,' I whispered to Justin as we descended towards Lhasa, 'life marches on, but I will always love you'. I realised I would never erase what had happened, but at least I could now live comfortably with my past. The memories of Justin and all my dead friends were no longer a burden I had to carry; rather, they were a warm, beautiful garden in my heart that I could access at any time, prompted or unprompted.

When, three days later, after interminable travel by jeep back to Kathmandu, I discovered that my crystal had gone, I reacted with philosophical calm. I believe my experience with the lama and the crystal was my destiny. I was meant to meet Lama Tsongkhapa; he gave me his crystal to have as long as I needed it. Now, though I searched in vain for the missing gem, I felt like I had no more doubts or unanswered questions.

It did not matter that it was gone. It had done its work.

CHAPTER NINE

A DISTANT CORNER OF THE WORLD

From Tibet I flew back to Kathmandu, then took a short flight to Beijing, and finally travelled 30 hours on the Trans-Siberian railway, first class, one-way to Ulaanbaatar, capital of Mongolia. I'd often dreamed as a girl of galloping across the steppes of Mongolia, so when Kristjan Edwards introduced me to Christopher and Enkhe Gierke and they invited me to visit them at their summer camp in central Mongolia, I jumped at the chance.

Christopher was a German filmmaker who had been making documentaries about Mongolia for the past decade. He also had a company that supplied cashmere products to French fashion titan Hermès. His wife was Mongolian, a descendant, no less, of Genghis Khan, and together with their young sons, Ich Tenger and D'Artagnan, they lived like nomads during Mongolia's brief summer months, spending the rest of the year in Nepal and France. I was excited by the prospect of spending a month in the Gierkes' camp on the Orkhon river in central Mongolia, having been invited to teach their staff to cook fine meals for the many international visitors they hosted during their summer sojourns.

I set out by jeep with one member of Christopher's staff for the camp that was seven hours' drive from Ulaanbaatar and arrived as the sun was beginning to set around 9.30 pm. As we got out and looked around, I stood, my heart leaping out of my chest and my mouth slightly open with wonder, and took in the eerily beautiful light. I could feel the crisp, clear air in my nostrils and on my skin. As far as I could see in every direction were darkly verdant hills and plains dotted with herds of yak, horses, sheep, goat and cattle. In the midst of this panoramic vista was the Gierkes' immaculate grouping of pristine white *gers*, nestled not far from a gently rushing river that sparkled like silver in the moonlight.

Christopher and Enkhe came out to greet me and I was struck immediately by this extraordinarily handsome couple: she with hair the colour of coals and cheekbones as sharp as corners, he with silver hair, voluptuous lips and a Teutonic air. They invited me to join them for dinner with their guests, a young Parisian couple.

Still dazed, I was led away to my *ger*, which was, to my amazement, five-star. I had three beds, a portable toilet, washbasin, fireplace, table, chairs and lots of decorative rugs, all creating an atmosphere of great cosiness. As I looked around I couldn't quite believe this was going to be 'home'. In fact, as I discovered with time, it just got better. I had my fire stoked for me every night before I went to bed; was woken with a cup of tea daily; and had a masseuse on call if I felt the slightest tension in my body after a day of hikes, riding and adventures. Obviously, this was not your run-of-the-mill nomadic existence—more like the Orkhon Hilton.

My dinner that night confirmed my suspicions that Christopher and Enkhe were the Mongolian equivalent of royalty as we sat down to a feast consisting of more offal than I have ever eaten in my life, all of it delicious, particularly the grilled livers. We washed it down with a great deal of vodka, beer and wine and as Christopher and Enkhe sniped at each other during the course of the evening, I got progressively more sozzled.

When my hostess, who had hitherto focused her attention on her Parisian visitors, turned on me and bluntly asked, 'Why don't you settle down and have children instead of gallivanting all over the world?', I sobered up quickly, suddenly apprehensive about spending a month in the company of someone as brusque as Enkhe appeared to be. Stung by her remark, I felt tempted to reply that there was nothing I would like better than to do what she suggested; but the thought of falling in love with another man after Justin was something I still struggled with. Instead, I held my tongue and beat a hasty retreat after a meal so good I couldn't help wondering why my hosts felt their camp needed my culinary skills.

The next morning, I made a mental note to try to acclimatise myself to local drinking habits, but barely had time to register the extent of my hangover when I was swept up in the preparations for a three-day hunting expedition for nuts and berries. Christopher, Enkhe and the boys, the Parisian couple and I settled in to one enormous four-wheel drive while Serge the chef, Tsorg the driver and at least a dozen Mongolians followed in a second jeep with a mountain of camping gear. We were off traversing the plains to a forest four hours away where fruits were ripe for picking.

I found myself entranced by the natural beauty of the woodlands and floral colour everywhere, the icy rivers and streams, the natural scenery that Christopher, Tsorg and I tramped through in search of an extinct volcano, a picturesque clearing or a breathtaking lookout point. I went hiking in surrounds so unspoiled it made my heart soar. The power of nature's beauty permeated my senses and I lapped up the sensation of being free in such wide, open spaces.

As a result of that expedition, I will also never take for granted a helping of pine nuts in a salad dressing or pesto, and now completely understand why they tend to be so expensive. It is indeed an arduous business getting them from the forests to the supermarket, as I quickly learned.

While most of the children went searching for berries, and returned much later with faces covered in purple splotches, I got into the nut-picking swing of things as we spread through the pungent pine forests combing for cones we could tease down from the trees' high branches. When finally we'd collected enough, we roasted the cones over a fire in order to extract the nuts. Then, once the nuts were removed, the next step was to prise the nuts from their shell and peel away the skin.

None of these tasks was simple; in fact, if I had been a professional being paid for my work, I would have earned practically nothing because I broke most of my nuts as I tried to bite, scratch, pull or prise them out of their shells with a knife. Then I gouged dents and holes

in the nuts with my fingers as I removed their skins. All
in all, it was an exhausting business requiring patience
and focus.

Serge continued to serve impressive meals for our
group during our time away, often deliciously seasoned
soups of mutton and noodles that always hit the spot.
Again, the thought crossed my mind that my culinary
skills might be redundant here, but I really didn't care. I
was too happy. As our large group sat around the
campfire eating, drinking and laughing, I closed my eyes
and relished the sense of contentment I felt.

On our return to the *ger* camp things only got better,
despite the background noise of Christopher and
Enkhe's ongoing bickering. The pair may have loved
their children and each other, but their strong
personalities locked horns endlessly, often flaring into
outbursts that didn't diminish despite the presence
of guests. I would watch with fascination as they
argued with each other, but afterwards, sitting with
Enkhe and comisserating about her father's illness,
I saw a different, softer side to this tempestuous wife
and mother.

When I needed to escape, I would typically jump on a
horse, joining a couple of Gierke horsemen on daily
sorties every morning after breakfast, steadily growing
in confidence as my horse and I galloped for longer
stretches and grew accustomed to one another as the
days passed. Here, thankfully, there were no roads,
traffic lights or police, telephone poles or Internet cafes,

bazaars or shopping malls, villages or settlements—not even fences—just kilometres and kilometres of savannah, rolling hills, river tributaries, forests and, always, radiantly blue skies that belied the lack of heat. Average temperatures in summer were roughly 15°C during the day; at night, they sank to freezing point. I wondered what it would be like to live here in the winter and understood better why the only people who did were constantly on the move.

For me, it was a sheer delight to find myself finally living my dream—the reality every bit as thrilling as the fantasy. In the wide open spaces I would canter or trot for hours and barely see a human being or a change in the valley's contours. As the wind swept through my hair, the sun's rays kissed my cheeks and my horse and I thundered over countryside where so few people had been, I felt alive and excited.

I'd return to camp, breathless and heart pumping, totally exhausted and exhilarated by the sense I had of being somewhere so remote that only marmots and eagles witnessed my expeditions. I knew this was something special and made a point of storing the ecstatic feeling to relive again in the future.

Sometimes we'd see nomads on horseback or spot a temporary *ger* settlement. Almost always, my fellow riders would insist on stopping to visit these 'neighbours' and I would sigh inwardly in anticipation of the inevitable ritual. We would call out respectfully from outside the *ger* if no one was visible; be ushered inside, and then small talk would begin in a language that sounded alarmingly like someone was choking. I would then be invited, by means of a charade of gestures and signals, to join them in a refreshing draught of … uh-oh, here we go again … fermented mare's milk.

In Australia, people tend to socialise over a glass of wine or beer; in Italy espresso is ubiquitous; and in Russia, it's vodka until everyone falls down. On the Mongolian steppes, every self-respecting nomadic family has a large barrel of *airag* at the ready and family and visitors make a point of consuming it on a daily basis, so that maintaining supply remains a full-time job. Local etiquette requires that if you walk past the barrel, you give the draught a thoroughly good stir.

What does it taste like? Well, not as ghastly as it sounds, but not so good either. And the fermentation process sure gives it a kick, as my hangovers over the ensuing days testified. After weeks in Mongolia however, whether from genuine appreciation or dire necessity (I'm not sure), I grew accustomed to the taste and even found myself occasionally hankering for a refreshing draught or two. What did my granny always used to say? 'It's amazing how we humans can adapt and accustom ourselves to almost anything.'

After a couple of weeks, the young Parisian couple left and I was delighted to see the back of them; I've seldom seen people so surly when everyone around them was doing their best to entertain and amuse. I grew up believing that it was polite to 'sing for your supper', something the grumpy Parisians conspicuously failed to do. I was so grateful to find myself with nothing to do but ride horses, go for long, beautiful walks at sunset, and be pampered in-between that I felt I had to contribute somehow. It was abundantly clear that the Gierke chef did not need my assistance, but I struck a bargain with Christopher and Enkhe: I would teach the staff how to bake biscuits and cakes and I would throw in a few English lessons, too.

Because of this, I found myself in the kitchen *ger* most afternoons, rustling up flourless chocolate cakes and Anzac biscuits before a small audience who, though completely silent, seemed to take avid interest in my demonstrations. We all certainly enjoyed tasting the final product. Was it my imagination, or was it the surroundings that made everything taste so scrumptious?

In turn, I also ventured where I had never gone before in terms of my own personal tastes and learned new methods of food preparation. I was mesmerised one day to witness a sheep being slaughtered for a feast that would have made Enkhe's forefathers proud. Fascinated, I watched as a couple of Christopher's men straddled an animal. One of them made a small slit in the sheep's belly, popped his hand through and ripped out the animal's aorta, thus ensuring a quick and relatively bloodless death. First checking the sheep's eyes for signs of life, one of the men began skinning it, starting at the neck and then along the throat, down each leg and along the centre of the belly. Once done, each leg was broken at the hock and the stomach, intestines and organs removed before the remaining carcass was cut up. The heart and lungs were scooped out, and the blood stored for the making of blood sausage.

The sheep pieces were not left to hang out for very long; all the sheep was to be cooked and eaten, fresh, within 24 hours. The dogs were fed the oesophagus and the eyes, while the contents of the large intestine, to my dismay, were carefully collected and stored in a jar. When I asked to what purpose this would be put, no one would answer until eventually Enkhe's mother said, giggling, in broken English, 'for medicine'. I wondered!

At dinner that night, guests were offered the choice of grilled or boiled offal. While Genghis Khan apparently preferred his boiled, I opted to have mine grilled and, over the ensuing weeks, sampled lung, heart, tongue, kidneys, liver, stomach lining, blood sausage, white sausage, intestines and brains. Characteristically, the spread would open with 'Khan soup', a dish of small boiled pieces of mutton and herbs served in a sheep's large intestine. Delicious! It was also not unusual for the household to enjoy fresh fish for dinner, usually mouth-watering trout caught in the nearby rivers. I would often sit on a rock with a picnic lunch during my riding forays and watch the rod fishermen catch up to 20 trout an hour.

My month passed dreamily by and as anticipated, all manner of guests descended during the summer, mainly from Europe, and this usually precipitated expeditions to the rivers and forests to go fishing or kayaking; closer to home, we would occasionally stage more conventional polo 'tournaments'. With Kristjan's help, Christopher had introduced polo to the natives of central Mongolia, so when we had enough people for two teams and could each throw in US$10 for a prize, we'd climb on our horses and thwack our mallets until the final whistle blew. I found it initially difficult as a left-hander to slouch on my horse, poised to hit the ball with my right hand, as per the rules, but with time and a little determination, I grew more dexterous and was able to occasionally hit a goal, much to Christopher's delight.

I had by now become part of the Gierkes' extended family, keeping Enkhe company as she tended her father who was slowly dying of cirrhosis of the liver, or joining Christopher and his sons in a tea ceremony where we imbibed the most expensive teas in the world from the most exquisitely refined tea cups. I sometimes thought there would be no end to the novel experiences and rituals to which I was being introduced and constantly felt deeply, humbly grateful for this extraordinary couple's hospitality.

Occasionally, foolishly, I would join the Mongolians on their drinking binges and wake up, sad and sorry, for not having noticed that I had consumed what seemed like three litres of *airag* in one night. On these days, the outdoor adventures would be jettisoned and I would lie in bed, whimpering, soothed only by another appetising broth of mutton and vegetables served up by Serge and a post-lunch massage by the resident masseuse. It was a pampered life and there were none more indulged than the young Gierke boys, who on the first day of school in early September were presented with gifts by their parents. First, Christopher made a speech about learning and made an offering in front of the *ovoo* (cairn for the gods). Then, he presented his younger son D'Artagnan with a beautiful black and brown horse while Ich Tenger, the elder, was given a state-of-the-art video and digital camera. Both kids were home-schooled by their parents and would spend a couple of hours each morning and afternoon inside their *ger* with Christopher and Enkhe teaching them maths and English.

The boys introduced me to Harry Potter, yet despite my enthusiasm for the tales of the wizard, they far preferred spending time with me dribbling and kicking soccer balls. Not surprisingly, with all this activity, I usually found myself tired at the end of the day. Most nights, Christopher, Enkhe and I would entertain fly-fishing enthusiasts from Finland; Ulaanbaatar-based embassy staff from Germany, Russia or China; or film crews from places as far afield as Paris and Pamplona, all looking to capture wilderness adventures on celluloid. It was a busy, active and sociable month that sped by all too quickly.

I felt twinges of disconsolation as I considered the unique world and lifestyle to which I would be bidding adieu. I galloped a few last times on my snowy polo mare and stopped with my fellow riders to play finger games—a ridiculously simple diversion similar to rocks, scissors, paper where the loser after 'best of three' sculls *airag* and the winner is the one left standing semi-sober. I would sit in my fermented mare's milk fog with a queasy smile on my face, throwing rocks at the wild dogs that barked ceaselessly on the edges of our campsite, and let my thoughts wander.

I still missed my darling Justin so much, as well as my wonderful, colourful, crazy buddies Paddy and Nato, but I recognised that I felt human again. I knew I was accepting the losses more with each passing day and could sense the quantum shift in my feelings since I had landed in Sri Lanka nine months before.

I still had not entirely let go of Justin, but I was glad that I had not forced or rushed things and instead, had just let things happen in time, my way. The grieving process—coming to terms with suffering and the 'letting go'—was not something that could be forced. It was something deeply personal and individual. When someone says, 'You need to move on', it's like a slap in the face. Of course, you know that at some stage you will have to 'move on', but it's so condescending when someone says it who is not in your shoes.

People are full of advice when you're grieving—and a lot of it hurts. So many people seemed to think that, in my case for example, my friendship with Justin's family, especially his mother Jan, was an unhealthy relationship that would only generate more pain for both of us. How wrong they were! Both of us had lost a man we loved; we offered each other so much understanding and solace. We had become close friends and knew our friendship would last forever.

And now I had the company of my friend Melon to look forward to. Melon had been working like a maniac back home in Australia and had recently resigned from her job. When I invited her to join me on the second half of my Mongolian trip, she didn't hesitate. We knew each other well from our university days; she expected me to arrange an unforgettable holiday in one of the world's last great frontiers and I knew she would handle anything I threw at her.

Like me, Melon was adventurous and 'can do'; it was what I loved most about her. So by the time I left the Gierkes, I was consumed with impatience to see Melon again. After months of travelling solo, I could barely wait to share my thoughts and experiences with a close, dear friend.

Mongolia's capital, Ulaanbaatar, is a sprawling, laid-back potpourri of old and new influences. It's not uncommon to see people in traditional dress strolling through the bazaars and streets, and many locals still live in traditional circular felt *gers* on the outskirts of the city along the river, Tuul Gol, which winds it ways through this increasingly modernised metropolis. Surrounded by picturesque mountains and a somewhat polluted sky, the city's urban landscape is dominated by Soviet-style high-rise apartment blocks built between the 1930s and 1970s. Tragically, much of the city's Buddhist roots have largely disappeared after the bloody purges of Soviet rule in the 1930s that saw thousands of monks arrested and countless monasteries and shrines destroyed. The monastery, Gandan Khiid, in the city centre is one of the only surviving temples of the 'feudal period'—all religious worship and ceremonies were outlawed in Mongolia until the Soviet Union fell apart in the early 1990s.

Since then, Buddhism has re-emerged as the spiritual path of choice, offering some solace to the country's two and a half million inhabitants who, despite their uniquely peaceful transition from Russian satellite state to independent nation, are struggling to find their economic feet. Elderly people still feel the loss of security that the former Russian old-age pension provided. Following the collapse of Soviet rule, social welfare has crumbled, resulting in increasing numbers of nomads drifting to the cities. One-third to one-half of Mongolia's population resides in the capital, where unemployment is close to 40 per cent, sometimes driving inhabitants to return to the rural areas to take up farming again. Many citizens leave the country seeking a better life. In fact, more Mongolians live outside Mongolia than in it—almost three and a half million live in China, and one million in Russia. One result of the rising poverty is the presence of street children who live in the city's underground sewers and heating pipes—the only place a person can survive in winter temperatures of −30°C.

The day Melon and I were reunited, I fell prey to one of these desperate street urchins, losing my wallet with over US$500 in cash just as we were preparing for our visit to Khövsgöl Nuur, an alpine lake on the Russian–Siberian border. Thankfully, I didn't lose my passport, but I still had the bother of reporting and replacing my credit card losses, not to mention losing all my spending money for a couple of weeks. I tried to be philosophical and think of it as a charitable donation to the Mongolian street kids, knowing that whoever had taken it would have sufficient *togrog* (Mongolian currency) to live a very comfy life for some time to come.

Despite this glitch, I was terribly excited to see Melon again, who assured me she was in dire need of 'a bloody good rest'. She then promptly shopped till she dropped in the capital's bazaars, practically hyperventilating with excitement at the affordability of the cardigans, shawls, overcoats, leatherwork, cashmere and camelhair products on offer. Once I had sorted out my financial woes, I ducked into one of the city's Internet cafes, caught up on my correspondence and ensured everything was on track for our flight to the lake the next day.

Swiftly, Melon was introduced to travel, Mongolian-style. After a hair-raising ride by taxi to the airport during which I again found myself closing my eyes, we fought with MIAT (Mongolian Airlines) officials about tariffs, noting rather pointedly that we were the only travellers being charged for excess luggage. Was it a coincidence that we were the only foreigners too? Then the flight was delayed by ten hours because, apparently, there was some visible cloud—a fairly uncommon occurrence in a country known as the 'land of blue sky'. We settled in, resigned, and played card games till our hearts, clubs, diamonds and spades threatened to go on strike.

Finally, it was time to board and it was everyone for themselves as Melon followed my cue and bolted aboard, elbows out, to ensure we got a good seat. From experience, one learns to try to hunt down a seat that does boast a seatbelt (not that anyone will ever tell you to belt up, mind you) and that doesn't flip back when you lean against your headrest.

Once we were settled, Melon's eyes grew huge as she watched five men disappear into the cockpit and the other passengers subsequently informed us, via sign language and broken English, that a freak snowstorm had deposited a lot of ice on the runway. Without the usual comforting rituals of flight attendant announcements or even a safety card in the seat pocket, Melon and I grimaced at each other nervously as our plane emitted ominous rumbles.

Miraculously we landed in one piece some 90 minutes later. No one informed us where in Mongolia we had landed so we had no way of knowing if this was our stop. But when the five men emerged from the cockpit reeking of alcohol, we decided to disembark. Shakily, we descended to a strip of tarmac in the middle of a paddock where berry-hawking locals assailed us, and discovered that we had, mercifully, arrived. At this news, we hauled our backpacks off the plane and started looking around for a driver from the lakeside camp we were visiting.

An hour later, under a full moon, we arrived at our camp in Khatgal on the edge of the region's fabled alpine lake and fell to sleep in *gers* stoked toasty warm in anticipation of our arrival. When we awoke to a crisp, cold morning and clear blue skies and took in our surroundings, Melon and I knew instantly that we were in the right place to rest our bodies and nourish our souls.

Surrounded by mountains, thick pine forest and lush meadows dotted with grazing yaks and horses, Khövsgöl Nuur is the second largest lake in Central Asia and one of the areas largest sources of fresh water, covering 2760 square kilometres. Home to argali sheep, ibex, bear, sable and moose, the region also boasts several unique tribes, including the legendary Tsaatan people, who I learned from my trusty *Lonely Planet* guide, are 'named from the Mongolian word for reindeer, *tsaa*. Their entire existence is based around the reindeer, which provide milk, skins for clothes, transport and, occasionally meat.' They live in *gers* in the forests surrounding the lake.

For five magical days, in this gorgeous setting, Melon and I hiked and rode and picnicked and slept. We read books, wrote in our diaries and caught up on each other's lives. Slowly, my friend began to shrug off her corporate stresses and bit by bit yielded to the pleasures of long gallops on horseback; scrumptious outdoor picnics with bread so good we had to write down the recipe; wonderful hot showers at the end of the day to soak away the rigours of exertion; and, finally, tasty evening meals with other foreigners, each with his or her own outlandish life story, toasted with fine Bordeaux.

I explained to Melon that this was the glamorous part of the month. For the rest of our time together, we would be in the hands of people recommended to me by others, so I couldn't be sure what to expect. I could only tell Melon that we were going to live and work with nomads in the Gobi desert for a week or two; and after that, we were flying to remote Western Mongolia to attend, among other things, an eagle-hunting festival. Melon nodded happily at all of this, excited at the surprises that awaited us.

When we arrived in Sainshand, gateway to the Gobi, roughly a week later, we couldn't have asked for a more striking contrast to our glamorous introduction to Mongolian life. After fighting back the need to dry-retch from the smells of greasy mutton and the other delights of our ten-hour train journey, Melon and I found ourselves abandoned at the railway station like orphans. Our euphoria after days of royal treatment in pristine wilderness up north was completely shattered and I frantically made phone calls to various pals of Christopher's who might be able to help.

Long after midnight, some locals finally arrived to pick us up, none of them speaking a word of English, and dumped a pretty desperate Melon and me in a shack for the night. Smelling to high heaven of mutton and horse's milk, with children asleep on mattresses on the floor, this small abode appeared to be someone's home. Melon and I, too tired to care, unfurled our mattresses and prepared to join the rest of the prostrate bodies on the floor.

After a surprisingly good night's sleep, we awoke to a long, trying day. Various emissaries transported us from pillar to post without ever being able to tell us where we were going or why. Melon and I unpacked our backpacks three times in muddled confusion under the misguided notion that this was where we were settling for the day. Eventually, around midnight, I heard two names I recognised from the list that Christopher had given me—Poorosarung and Erdenbillag. Melon and I introduced ourselves to the couple with sign language, packed our things, and then all four of us sped off into the ink-black night by jeep. At 2.30 am, we stopped and pitched a tent in darkness, sipped a cup of tea, nibbled a stale piece of pastry, and fell asleep.

When Melon and I popped our heads through the tent flaps the next morning we were greeted by a small posse of camels, goats, sheep and horses, standing quietly like obedient schoolchildren and staring at us with polite curiosity. Once we got over that surprise we stepped out, looked around and saw … nothing, absolutely nothing, as far as the eye could see.

Not a tree, not a hill, not a rock, not a *ger*, not a rabbit. There was not, as far as we could see, a single living thing in the middle of this wilderness other than our delightful hillbilly guides, the herd, Melon and me.

CHAPTER TEN
LIVING AS THE NOMADS DO

Mesmerising days followed in the Gobi desert that would be impossible to forget. Not for nothing are Mongolians known as 'the people of five animals'. Most Mongolian children learn to ride before they can walk and, accompanied by our guides, married couple Erdenbillag and Pooroosarung, or Billygoat and Pooro as we fondly nicknamed them, Melon and I rode horses and camels, milked cows and herded goats and sheep. Essentially, our task was to take Billygoat and Pooro's small herd of 40 double-humped camels, 30 sheep, 20 goats and 40 cows from summer to winter camp. It was the end of summer now and the colder months were approaching.

However, while the pair had doubtless done this trip before, not a day seemed to pass in which we did not get lost. Or, perhaps, it was simply Melon and I who frequently felt dazed—attributable no doubt, to excessive *airag* we consumed around the potbelly stove at night.

After long, crazy days of bouncing around in our jeep or horse riding Mongolian-style (standing straight in the saddle), hunting wild deer or chasing recalcitrant camels, we'd play charades under the stars at day's close, sing songs or challenge one another to a few dozen more rounds of finger games before retiring for the night. At first, Melon and I were shocked by the lack of inhibition Billygoat and Pooro exhibited in our company as they burped, farted, picked their noses, slurped and spat, but as time passed, it became harder to muster a critical eye. Melon and I would give each other the once-over and realise we were every bit as smelly and as dirty as our friends, we just hadn't yet acquired the habit of picking our noses in company.

Certainly, aroma de boiled mutton seemed to be the order of the day. But what days they were: clear blue skies and miles and miles of nothing, offering Melon and me a unique opportunity to empty our brains and fill up our hearts. Days would blend into each other as we set out on horseback to find fossil evidence of dinosaurs that once roamed across the stony, scrubby wasteland. At other times, we'd yell with excitement when we'd spot wild gazelles clip-clopping on the horizon or spy hawks wheeling in the sky. Very occasionally, we'd bump into other Mongols also moving camp and then, sure as night follows day, there'd be plenty of socialising and swigging at the barrel of milk.

On our last evening in the Gobi wilderness, we hit a new low when both Melon and I awoke, still fully dressed, on top of our sleeping bags, covered in *airag* detritus and unable to remember a single thing about the previous night. Obviously, it was time to return to civilisation before we began to take seriously the various marriage proposals that had come our way on our wild safari.

Both Melon and I found ourselves overwhelmed with sadness at bidding our new friends farewell. Billygoat and Pooro had been more than hospitable and we couldn't imagine that we'd ever have the opportunity to repay the kindness. Hugging them for the last time and waving furiously, we climbed aboard another scary plane, this time bound for Olgii in western Mongolia.

The point of going to Olgii was to climb the Tavan Bogd mountain, where you can look out from its height of 4374 metres to neighbouring China and Russia. After a snowstorm that made our flight even more daunting than usual (if it were possible), we landed in the capital of the Bayan-Olgii province to be assaulted by weather colder than we had yet experienced. We also soon discovered that we were among a completely new kind of Mongolian tribe.

In fact, as we learned, most of Olgii's inhabitants are not Mongolian at all, but descendants of Kazakh nomads who roamed Central Asia for hundreds of years before settling in the mid-nineteenth century. They came to graze their sheep on the high mountain pastures during summer and those who stayed upheld their unique culture, so that Kazakh customs in Mongolia today are far more intact than in Russian-influenced Kazakhstan.

The culture is quite different from Mongolia's own; Kazakh saddles are a different shape and Kazakh *gers* are more richly decorated. Their religion is Muslim, a rather loose Sunni Islam that sometimes turns a blind eye to the drinking of vodka, while the language is Turkic and more closely aligned to Russian than to Mongolian.

Thanks to my network of friends in Asia, we stayed with a Kazakh family for three days and nights. Despite the family's kindest intentions and central heating provided by a potbelly fire stoked with yak dung, we nearly froze to death inside the family's beautifully decorated *ger*. Wiser (and distinctly sleep-deprived) after this experience, I turned down the family's suggestion that we camp overnight on the mountain when we began discussing our next sortie. Melon and I were both usually more than willing to bite off more than we could chew, but even we drew the line at sleeping in a tent in −10°C temperatures!

Instead, we set off on horseback with a gas cooker, picnic and guide for a day's riding to get as close as we could to the Tavan Bogd summit. Departing at around 8 am, we hiked through enchanting, dazzling valleys of deep snow, surrounded by towering mountains and piercing blue skies — one of the first things we spotted was a sign graphically depicting the presence of snow leopards and bears. Silenced by the thought and hushed by the otherworldly atmosphere, we ascended the mountain slowly on horseback, carefully picking our way over streams of ice and avoiding marmot holes. We were never exactly sure where our horses would put down their hooves next; what would make them shy; or when it was time for us to climb down as they manoeuvred their way over treacherously glistening terrain. Occasionally, the snow was so deep and the passes so risky, we'd trudge through on foot, following our friendly guide.

In this eerily beautiful, snow-muffled ambience, with only the crunch of horses' hooves and the occasional click of a stirrup to disturb the silence, we ascended the mountain more and more slowly as the rise became steeper and the snow deeper. The sun cast long silhouettes on the virgin snow as we continued to slowly forge forward.

By 3 pm, we'd reached the mountain's infamous 19-kilometre long Potanii Glacier and we knew we had to stop. This was like no other glacier I had seen before and it looked every bit as dangerous as its reputation. Snaking down the mountain between two ridges, it glistened menacingly, snowy crevasses tucked secretively all along its icy trunk. Professional mountain climbers were warned not to attempt climbing Potanii without the best equipment and years of experience; Melon and I were satisfied to just take in the view and wave to Kazakhstan to our left and China to our right. We sipped our noodle soup and toasted a spellbinding day.

Alas, the sense of enchantment rapidly dissipated as the sun dropped and the temperature plummeted. Suddenly, we realised how far we had come … and how far we had to go back.

As the extent of the dauntingly long trip ahead dawned on us, we tried to keep up our spirits and our body temperature by slapping our legs and gustily singing every song we knew—Australia's national anthem, school hymns, 'Scarborough Fair', anything.

This worked for a while but as the hours progressed and night fell, we were still riding in the cold, our singing waned and we fell into silence. I was cursing myself for not thinking about the return journey and drawing on every resource I had to not lose my fragile composure. Poor Melon, mute on the horse tramping in front of me, simply seemed to have frozen solid. By 9.30 pm, enduring cold and discomfort, I heard Melon's voice: 'Libby, I'm worried my feet are getting frostbite'.

I quelled the impulse to panic and suggested we climb down from our horses; walking would at least keep our blood circulating. Together we tramped alongside our equally wearied mares in the pitch-black, barely able to see the footsteps of our guide ahead. Interminable minutes, quarter and half hours followed where we imagined every sound, every pallid glistening, as an indication that we had reached our camp. It never was.

I cursed myself again and again for my stupidity. The guide had been unable to communicate with Melon and me while the pair of us, in any case, had been adamant that we wanted to reach the infamous Potanii Glacier at the very least. Now we were paying the price for our lack of foresightedness. Melon's terse 'I don't know how much longer I can go on,' made me realise that she, too, was using every bit of her energy to just keep going.

Eventually, just before midnight, the three of us limped into camp and threw ourselves on the potbelly stove. Melon and I wept with relief and exhaustion, not entirely convinced that our frozen appendages would ever defrost. With no energy to eat, drink, wash or change, we lay down on the blankets on the floor of the *ger* and settled in for another windy night. The next day, Melon didn't emerge until after lunch, but I went for a long hike to clear my head and later went riding on the flats. Both of us felt very thankful to have survived the night—turning back so late could very easily have been a fatal mistake.

Later in the day, Melon and I came across a sheep trapped in a frozen river. We decided we had to try and get it out and soon couldn't stop laughing as once again we found ourselves chattering in water cold enough to curdle your blood. Bless Melon, who rolled up her trousers, encased her legs in plastic bags and waded into the stream to hack at the ice that had snared the animal After many attempts, the sheep was finally freed.

Back in Olgii, we moved in with another Christopher connection, a regional police superintendent and his family, and were delighted to be back in relative luxury. There was even a decent bathroom and a hot tap in the shower! Melon and I hugged each other in glee until we realised that the bathroom facilities were purely ornamental; they looked good, but they didn't work. Melon and I sighed and resigned ourselves to rudimentary washbasin scrubs. Then, one night after supper, the superintendent's 16-year-old daughter asked us if we'd like a shower and we nodded vigorously. Before we knew it, the whole family had packed up and we were skedaddling along the dusty roads with them in the darkness.

Not long after, we were escorted into neon-lit public showers that were abuzz with the sort of excitement typical of a Saturday night hoedown in an Australian country town. Obviously, taking a shower was a major social event in Olgii—why else was the entire populace here backslapping, gossiping and laughing with one another? With not much socialising to do, Melon and I ducked into our shower cubicles and abandoned ourselves to the hot water.

Refreshed and back at home with our hosts, Melon and I agreed this was not your usual run-of-the-mill tourist jaunt and wondered what might be next on the agenda. So when the police superintendent announced that it was time for the annual Kazakh eagle-hunting festival about which we had heard so much, we just went with the flow.

Eagle hunting, we learned, is a Kazakh tradition dating back to Marco Polo and involves training the mighty birds to hunt marmots, rabbits, small foxes and wolves. Having caught them, the birds release their quarry to their trainers who club the prey to death, offering part of the meat to the eagle as reward.

We set off one morning with the family to witness the spectacle for ourselves and made our way by car along the only road out of Olgii, through endless valleys of barren, rocky landscape. Suddenly, Melon let out a startled yell and I muffled one myself when I saw what she saw: horsemen, clad top to toe in dark animal furs and skins, cantering past us in a slow procession on horses richly adorned with silver and coloured woven fabric. Many of the riders were wisened old men with long, whiskery beards. There were also several young boys emulating their deadpan elders as they galloped across the desolate valley floor in the direction of an enormous rocky hill.

Many of the men rode with one hand on the reins, the other in mid-air with a hooded eagle perched on the upheld arm. Considering the average weight of the female eagles used for hunting was 15–20 kilograms, it was amazing to think that some of these horsemen had been travelling in this fashion for five days to reach the festival site.

To our amazement, Melon and I found ourselves among friends on arrival. We had met so many nomads on our various travels over the past month, and sculled so much *airag* with them, that we were greeted happily by a lot of familiar faces. I couldn't help thinking that the only way to travel was to live the life of the people and to forget about the usual tourist hit list.

Even more surprising was the fact that we were not the only foreigners in this freezing, god-forsaken part of the world. A writer and photographer were present from *National Geographic*, as well as a couple of other foreign journalists. As it turned out, the Kazakh eagle hunters are a dying breed and Melon and I were about to witness something genuinely rare. This was no sideshow put on for visitors; it was the real thing, and everyone was intent on the competition ahead that would determine the champion hunter.

We watched transfixed under Mongolia's perennial blue sky as the eagle hunters climbed the rocky outcrop with their hooded birds and waited for the two-way radio call to signal the birds' release. Far below, a horseman trailed a hare as bait on a rope.

As each eagle was released the crowd held its breath, watching as the bird soared, then dived, occasionally snaring the hare in a magnificent swoop, at other times completely missing and flying off, sometimes away, not to be seen until much later. Sitting behind the judges' scoring table, Melon and I tried to fathom the criteria that determined the supremo eagle. Was it speed? Dexterity? Smoothness of flight? The bird's degree of murderous intent?

To this day, we are none the wiser, although we understood fully the import of winning the prize, as 50 or so nervous and excited black-garbed warriors came down from the mountain to hear the announcement. An American woman, dressed jarringly in stars and stripes, presented the trophy on behalf of a whisky company and handed over a cheque as cameras clicked and a television camera whirred.

But the day's events were not over. Two wild nomads took to their horses and, egged on by a pumped-up, macho crowd, conducted a hand-to-hand tug-of-war over a fox skin, which seemed to go on for hours. The spectators were on their feet roaring enthusiastically, while the contestants held on to the skin for dear life.

The festival's climax occurred at the end of the day and was enough to reduce animal lovers to tears. Once again, the hunters and their eagles returned to the top of the hill. Below, a lone, rangy wolf was tied to a stake. The radio signal was given and en masse, the eagles dived to peck the poor beast to death. Afterwards, the satisfied crowd proceeded to party on with vodka and boiled mutton after what they considered to be a fine day's entertainment.

We returned to Olgii, where Melon and I prepared to bid Kazakh life goodbye, and braced ourselves for yet another dodgy Mongolian flight before finally disembarking in Beijing. As our plane flew over the snowy wastes of Olgii en route to Ulaanbaatar, I laughed to myself. It was hard to believe I had once trembled at the prospect of a 50-minute Melbourne to Sydney flight on Qantas.

In Beijing, Melon and I prepared to part. She was going on to visit other parts of China solo; I was flying to Paris to re-immerse myself in the western world and was looking forward to the rest of my around-the-world trip.

But first we went together to Tiananmen Square to see for ourselves the site where the recent tragic events had taken place. By coincidence, our visit fell on the anniversary of Paddy and Nato's air crash. As Melon and I lit candles in remembrance of the mass student protest and ensuing bloodshed that had occurred here in 1989, I found my thoughts inevitably straying to my own personal losses.

Certainly, I had travelled many thousands of miles, literally and emotionally. Now I was on my way to France to cleanse my mind and lay to rest any unresolved pain. On the outskirts of Paris, I planned to join a ten-day meditative retreat. I hoped that this would not break me, as many people had suggested, but finally bring to a close another chapter of my life. Melon and I hugged each other goodbye; it was time for us to journey in different directions and, once again, I was striking out on my own.

CHAPTER ELEVEN
BACK IN WESTERN CULTURE

Will I have that Snickers bar? No, you better not ... you don't need it. Bugger it, have it, have the Bounty as well. Perhaps I should have a baguette au fromage? Hmmm, maybe all three. I could buy the Snickers and keep it for later. Oh what to do ...

These profound thoughts were going through my mind as I waited on a station platform at Gare de Lyon, Paris, for my train heading to Laroche Migennes, the nearest village to the Dhamma Mali Centre de Vipassana. I know it's hard to believe that I would willingly choose to stay silent for ten days—I grew apprehensive myself whenever I thought about it too much—but this was a challenge that appealed to me.

Friends, family and complete strangers had tried to warn me off the experience; the common attitude was that this would be one of the most daunting things I would tackle in my life. Ha! After what I'd been through in the last two years, not to mention the last couple of months, could a meditative retreat in the beautiful Burgundy region of France really be that scary?

I would find out soon enough, but there was no doubt that this was another important part of my journey. I didn't want to travel the world only to find that I had unfinished business. This meditative retreat would sort out any residual emotional baggage for me. Also, most importantly, I would learn to meditate! I knew myself well enough to realise that I would always pack my life with full-on experiences. I believed the act of meditation would be a useful tool to keep myself calm in the midst of all of it.

I arrived at the meditation centre after a three-hour journey feeling very much like I was attending my first day at school. Fired up, I followed the rest of the students who, like me, were enrolled to participate in the 10 days of silence. As I queued and checked in with the rest of the students I was handed a pouch and told to hand over my valuables, including any reading or writing materials. I was then assigned a number and bed, F3, and sent to meet my compatriots bunking with me in the dorm. We whispered our introductions, none of us sure if the 'noble code of silence' was yet in force. Swiftly, after brief chats, I had a snapshot of my fellow meditators.

F1 was an older German woman, taking her first break in 15 years from the stress of caring for her 19-year-old daughter who suffered obsessive compulsive disorder. F2 was a gorgeous looking 29-year-old, addicted to LSD for a decade and still struggling, after a year, to stay clean. F4 was a rebirthing therapist from the south of France, Marie-Hélène, searching to expand her mind with exposure to other therapies. F5, Sandrine, was a 35-year-old Rastafarian who made a living from nude modelling for artists in Provence. Finally, F6 was Miriam, a 54-year-old reformed alcoholic now practising Saufology, an alternative therapy that she explained worked with both the conscious and unconscious mind.

With barely enough time to digest these titillating accounts, we were summoned for formalities and some

50 people of both sexes listened avidly as the rules were spelled out. Firstly, we were to not talk for the entire ten days—no surprises there—and we were, furthermore, to refrain from any physical interaction (including eye contact) with any of our fellow students, male or female.

We were not allowed to read, write or run, only to walk within a roped area that, in effect, forced us to tread repetitively in a circle some 50 metres in circumference. No exercise was allowed, nor yoga, and we were asked to keep our eyes closed and to maintain one posture during the many hours of daily meditation. The rules and regulations seemed to go on for hours. I blanched and cursed inwardly.

We started the regime with a one-hour meditation the opening night, making ourselves comfortable in our allocated cells that were decorated with all manner of rugs and cushions. Thankfully, we would be allowed to meditate on a rug if we wished—and I wished. Some people were using their cushions like building blocks. One woman sat on her cushion like she was riding a horse (I later discovered she was a professional horse whisperer); another participant looked as though he was sitting on a riverbank fishing and drinking beer.

Each day began with a 4.30 am rise to immediately begin a two-hour meditation session. I would typically find myself slouched forward within half an hour, my head hanging with a puddle of drool in my lap, occasionally even waking myself with a start to discover I had been snoring.

Breakfast followed from 6.30 to 8 am—I would throw muesli and prunes down my throat and make a beeline back to my cell in the nearby dormitory block where I would sleep before the next meditation session. Sure enough, 8 am would come round all too quickly and for three hours, I would be fighting pins and needles, unsuccessfully trying to ignore aches all over my body.

Lunch between 11 am and 1 pm was definitely the highlight of each day. All forms of delicious rolls, baguettes and pastries were combined with plenty of lettuce, legumes and tasty, fresh vegetables, making the midday repast a welcome diversion. Then I would do a couple of dozen laps of the 50-metre circuit and spend the rest of the lunch break daydreaming, people-watching or simply gazing at the falling leaves.

Equally often, my mind would race so quickly and loudly that I almost expected others to comment on my litany of thoughts. During our silent rest periods, I would spend hours conjuring up life stories for the other students. I longed for pen and paper so I could write them down. I pictured myself handing these stories to my fellow meditators and discussing with them how close (or not) to real life my hypotheses about their lives were. I didn't only spend hours making up life stories; I also wrote letters in my head, designed outfits and concocted recipes … you name it, my mind was going there.

The three consecutive meditation sessions after lunch, for me, were excruciating. After five days, I found I could still my mind sufficiently to meditate for hours and emerge from a session refreshed. But it would not be inaccurate to say that I just as often simply wanted to slump over and sleep, or get up and stretch. My body seemed to be riddled with aches and pains; I was constantly distracted by the noises emanating from my fellow meditators. In the silence, every cough sounded like a road accident. As 50 acolytes digested their lunch of lentils, beans and various other legumes ... well you can imagine the rumbles and mumbles coming from four dozen stomachs, bowels and bottoms.

Then there were the snorts, sniffles and tears of those affected by the minutes, hours and days of silence as feelings began to well up. In my case, my feeling tank seemed to be almost empty—the thought crossed my mind, with some relief, that I had possibly emptied my personal store of tears. Instead, I would peek around in the muffled darkness at my fellow meditators. Every time I did this, I seemed to be the only recalcitrant because everyone else appeared engrossed in reflection. And to my horror, most were sitting perfectly upright. For a wriggler like myself, this was an achievement I could barely comprehend.

After a brief afternoon tea break (no dinner, alas) there were two more meditation sessions, broken up by a teacher discourse on Vipassana practice, and finally lights out at 9.30 pm. With such a routine, I swiftly realised there was nowhere to hide and seriously wondered if I would be able to last the distance. Being silent wasn't the problem, I discovered, but endless hours of meditation were. Then, just when I thought I couldn't take another second of it—my determination would kick in and I'd be counting off another day. Occasionally, I would find that the hours of meditative practice were working. My sessions were a rollercoaster: sometimes painfully aware, at other times I experienced a serene mindlessness from which I would emerge unable to believe that hours had passed without my conscious awareness.

When the ten days drew to an end and the code of silence was lifted, I barely knew how to react. I felt lobotomised; after so much time to think, my brain felt numb and talking was painful and slow. I floundered as I began conversations, words stumbling out of me like a prisoner walking free after months of captivity. Then tears started to roll down my cheeks as I expunged the last remaining vestiges of feeling—what a deflated balloon I was. I felt like I had survived deep brain surgery.

So much inward reflection had taken place that not talking was easier. There was almost no need to talk—we had all gone through such a personal exploration that to begin to explain the realisations seemed pointless. In the final analysis, the experience made me feel alone, but also self-sufficient and stronger than ever.

Before Vipassana, I was familiar with my personal vagaries; after ten days of this physical and mental endurance however, I felt certain I had faced everything about myself that I might have avoided up until then. Of course, one never knows 'what one doesn't know', but I couldn't help feeling that there was little left to fear.

Less than a day later I was on a train bound for Chamonix and was rereading, yet again, an email I had first received over two years ago from a stranger who had just heard (then) of Justin's death.

From: Riccardo Allodi
To: Libby Southwell
Sent: 6.42 am Thursday 14 March 14 2002
Subject: ciao

Hi Libby,

I just came back from Algeria, where I've worked for 40 days. It was very interesting, my first time in the Sahara desert.

Thank you very much for the PDF file about Justin. I miss him a lot; I would have liked to meet him again, as planned last year, in Chamonix where I head tomorrow. We would have spent a lot of time together skiing, partying or simply exchanging ideas, talking about everything over two beers.

I've known Justin for four to five months—a very short time considering that he was a mine of resources (confirmed by the articles you sent me written by his friends), a very friendly guy, simple and very nice, and a perfect companion for all situations—but also, enough time to realise how special he was.

I'm using the past form 'was' instead of 'is' ... that's wrong! He still is a great guy, someone who makes you think about shared experiences and conversations and who still has the power to be a lighthouse for projects in my life. For instance, the job I now have is one I started to consider seriously only last year after a lot of thinking. I was working as a research and development chemist in plastics in Italy at the time, something very normal with routines and little time for travel, friends or fun.

I quit that job in November 2000, moved to Chamonix and started to think about what I wanted to do with my life. I wanted to have projects and dreams for the future that excited me; and I did not want to feel that I was just letting time pass. I began thinking about working in oil fields where you travel around the world, meet people with different ways of thinking, traditions and cultures and different experiences; where you may work 30 days straight, but you then have a month off to realise other goals. And then finally, in December 2001, I got a job in the oil-rigging field. Justin and his philosophy of life had a role in all the thoughts and decisions I took to realise this dream.

Libby, it's very hard for you now, but Justin will always be present in your decisions and thoughts. He will give you a lot of strength and power, perhaps even more than before! This happened to me when I was 25 and I lost my father; today when I succeed in something important, I know it's also thanks to my father, and now also Justin, who have helped me along the way.

In April 2001, I lost another friend at Chamonix, a French guy called Julien. He died skiing a very dangerous couloir under the Mont Blanc; Justin met him as well. He and Julien were both free spirits; they enjoyed and lived their life much more than most other people do. They will always be present in my mind and my heart.

Keep in touch,

Riccardo

Whenever I read this letter from Riccardo, I felt touched by the warmth I felt emanating from his writing. I had never met this friend of Justin's in person, but after corresponding with him for almost two years, he was beginning to feel like a familiar, dear friend. Now, at last, we were meeting in Chamonix, and I was both excited and nervous.

So many friends had questioned my desire to visit Chamonix after all this time. Why did I want to go where Justin had been so happy? How would I feel? Did I want to bring it all up again? The truth was I didn't know how I would feel, but something called me to Justin's beloved mountains. I wanted to be with people like Riccardo who seemed to know the Justin I knew and who appeared to understand him so well.

And then there he was on the station platform, easy to recognise from various photographs we had exchanged. We hugged each other with relief, happy to meet each other at last. After my ten days of silence, I was finding it hard to find words, but I needn't have worried. As Riccardo and his brother, Marco, bundled me into their car and made me welcome in their rustically simple cottage on the outskirts of Chamonix, I began to relax.

Later, as the three of us rustled up a delicious pasta dish together in the kitchen and wolfed it down with red wine, I began to feel decidedly at home. I was also talking again like I hadn't for ages. It was such a relief to be able to share good memories of Justin with someone as uncomplicated as this skiing friend of his. Occasionally, when sitting in one of Justin's favourite bars in the skiing village, the weather closing in so that we had to reschedule one of our hikes, Riccardo and I would make a toast in Justin's honour. We'd ruefully commiserate with one another that Justin couldn't be with us in person to laugh, drink and anticipate another upcoming skiing season.

Justin had sent me a short story he'd written once about running in the mountains every day; and for the time I spent with Riccardo in Justin's beloved Chamonix, I too ran every day, setting out first thing in the crisply cold late November morning air. And instead of the mountains ripping my heart into a thousand pieces, I found my heart flowering with a sense of peace and joy.

Riccardo's heartfelt stories about how happy Justin had been here made me feel complete. I had an enormous sense of closure, knowing that I would be a different person again when (and if) I ever returned.

With less than a month to go before Christmas, which I planned to celebrate in Australia with my family, I embarked on a whistlestop tour of the globe. My first stop was New York, on the way to Philadelphia, where I was catching up with old friends, Hamish and Belle. The fabled Big Apple in the run-up to Christmas is reputedly magical and my visit lived up to expectations; after an especially severe snowstorm on the eve of my arrival the festive decorations glittered brilliantly against a dark and brooding backdrop.

Walking down the streets of Manhattan, it was hard to take in anything around me as snow whipped my face. Casting my eyes downwards all I saw of New York was steam vapour rising from manholes, the brooms of street sweepers brushing litter into pans, and the blur of yellow cabs as they purred past.

I shivered with excitement at all this urban frenzy and went in search of a Greyhound bus. My 'Noo Yoik' experience would not be complete without a bus journey to somewhere: I wanted to close my eyes, lean against the window and imagine I was Julia Roberts in *The Pelican Brief.*

When the enormous woman at the Greyhound window told me the ticket to Philadelphia would cost US$70, I hesitated, trying to quickly compute if catching a train was a better alternative. The big mama behind the ticket window turned to her co-worker and, one caustic eye on me all the while, proclaimed loudly. 'Marla, can you believe this? Now we're supposed to wait while she figures out what's she gonna do ...' I didn't know whether to bite back or laugh—I definitely wasn't in Tibet any more!

Mildly stunned by the impatience I found so foreign after months in countries where time was a friend, I bought my ticket, climbed aboard the bus and plonked myself up the front where a female passenger had started a one-sided conversation with the driver. 'Praise the Lord, God love you, I lost my brother in 9/11 and I'm aching and paining, but you are driving so well, God bless you and thank you Ma'am.'

The driver and I exchanged glances and didn't say a word. When later efforts at conversation met with a wall of silence, the woman finally settled quietly in her seat as we coasted along the freeways.

Pop. Pop. POP.

In the silence, the explosions from a gum-chewing passenger sounded as loud as machine-gun fire. I shrugged inwardly and gazed out the window, daydreaming.

Pop. Pop. POP. POP.

Suddenly, our bus came to a screaming halt on the side of the highway and our driver, a woman the size of a

back in western culture

small house, turned to the passengers, one hand on her waist, the other flailing furiously in the air. 'Right! We're not going any further. You come to the front and you tell me who you are. If I hear one more pop! You hear me? You're driving me crazy!'

There were various mutters and mumbles all round, but the gum-popper failed to 'fess up and we soon got back on our way. About ten minutes later, there was another soft 'pop' from the rear, but if anyone heard it but me, no one let on.

Again, I found myself contrasting the Western way with the Asian way of life. When you jump on a bus in India, everyone seems a little crazy but it's the bus driver who's the craziest, while no one seeking conversation would ever meet silence—the atmosphere aboard any public transport is like a bustling market. In the States on the other hand, as in many Western countries, everyone keeps to themselves and anyone who steps outside his or her boundaries—beware.

At the bus depot, Hamish and Belle swept me into a welcoming embrace and took me off to their house in Amish country. For four days I built snowmen, played ice hockey, decorated fir cones, stuffed the turkey and sat around with friends and celebrated Thanksgiving. For me, it was easy to give thanks: life had never seemed so easy, or so relaxed. As we all raised our glasses to propose a toast, I found myself looking forward to future celebrations.

Then, I was off again, this time to the Bahamas to see Justin's brother, Alistair, via Washington and Miami. I left New York in a scary blizzard that caused dozens of flights to be cancelled but luckily, not mine. As my fellow passengers and I walked out on to the tarmac in the wind and sleet I heard the pilot telling a flight attendant that flying conditions were 'pretty rough'. I immediately became worried, needing very little to ignite my dismay about the perils of flying. As we waited for the plane to be defrosted, I sat with clammy hands—frustrated to see how easily I became anxious. But the flight was uneventful and soon I was in the arms of my surrogate family—Justin's brother and his wife, Harriet.

Justin's death was an unforgettable loss, but it brought me closer to his family. I will never forget being in his parents' sitting room the day after Justin died; Justin's parents sat on either side of me, each holding my hand and, their own unbearable pain notwithstanding, tried to comfort me as I wept. 'You will be happy again,' Justin's mother said, her husband nodding in agreement, 'and we will be the first to celebrate your happiness'. Despite the blur of my tears and emotions, I was struck then by their selflessness. This sense of closeness only intensified when Jan and I went to New Zealand a few weeks later for Justin's inquest, the pair of us numb with grief as we waited our turn in the Christchurch court.

Two inquests were first in line, the first confirming the death of a Canadian cyclist killed by a motorist in front of her husband. Horror-struck at the thought of what that must have felt like for the husband, Jan and I clenched each other's hands.

The second inquest made me angry, as the judge appeared to be blaming a mother for texting her son by mobile phone. The son had responded to the message while he was driving and in doing so, had crashed into the back of a truck, dying instantly. Tears were rolling down the mother's face; it was awful to watch. That night, drinking our whiskies, we absorbed the events of the day, and I knew then that Jan was going to be a trusted friend for the rest of my life.

Quite often, her sons felt closer to me than my own brother. We could now talk about Justin ('Blockie' to his brothers) calmly, sad that he was gone, but happy with our memories. 'I loved Blockie so much,' Alistair said as he, Harriet and I talked one evening about how each of us had dealt with the news of Justin's death. Each of us adored different aspects of him; and felt the sadness of losing something special in our lives. We were wistful and melancholic, but also philosophical and accepting.

My days in the Bahamas glided past in a haze of yachts, sunsets, barbecues and calypso music. The sun kissed my skin; the salt water massaged my body; the atmosphere soothed my senses. I was happy again and it must have showed because Alistair's male friends began to circle. At a beach picnic one of his pals grabbed me in a frenzy of passion, hugging me a little closer than felt comfortable, telling me what a truly wonderful woman I was.

'I'm so sorry to step outside the boundaries,' he said politely in his Dutch accent, 'but I really wanted you to know how I feel'.

A few days later, finally making my way back to Australia for Christmas, I met a very handsome man at Miami's international airport who started talking to me in the waiting lounge before embarkation. On the flight, he asked me to join him at the back of the aeroplane and we talked for hours. Paul told me about himself— European-born and based, aviation industry, divorced, loved his children, a long-time girlfriend, flying on business—and I told him the story of Justin and the fact that I was not ready for a relationship.

Later, as we disembarked, he asked me to wait for him after passing through immigration, and I did. We made small talk as we waited for our luggage and together strolled out of the airport. He gave me his card with his contact details, and asked me to look him up the next time I was in Europe. 'Close your eyes for a minute Libby,' he said suddenly. I did and felt my hands being taken in his and his lips pressed gently to mine.

I was like a Christmas tree suddenly lit up, voltage coursing through my veins. Speechless, legs shaking, heart pounding, I managed to exchange some farewell pleasantries and walked off in a daze.

I never saw Paul again, but that night, as I fell asleep, for once I did not fantasise about Justin. Instead, I tossed and turned thinking about the handsome executive and finally, before falling to sleep in the wee hours, admitted to myself that I was maybe ready—two years on—for another relationship.

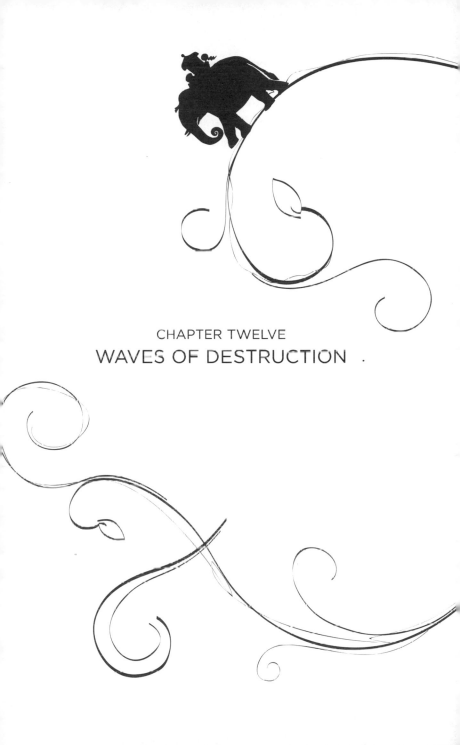

CHAPTER TWELVE
WAVES OF DESTRUCTION

As the new year approached I was feeling optimistic and excited. Most of all, I looked forward to returning to Serendip—I was missing the colour and chaos of the island republic. My brief Christmas break in Australia had provided an unsettling contrast to life in Sri Lanka: Sydney seemed full of air-conditioned super malls where every single trolley worked, the choice of foods was dizzying and you needed a genius IQ to find your car in the parking lot. On the roads, traffic was worse than in Colombo's peak hour despite state-of-the-art equipment in perfect working order operating around the clock to keep motorists in check. Back in Colombo, I'd typically hail a *tuk-tuk* and hold my breath as the driver manoeuvred his way through potholes and around buses, cheek-to-jowl with other honking taxis, cars, trucks and drivers. It was crazy fun and you always arrived quickly, cheaply and somehow in one piece.

Australian and Sri Lankan lifestyles were different in other ways, too. In Sydney, I noticed a fashion-consciousness that bordered on the competitive. Who was the most fashionable? Who was the coolest? I'd check out the passing parade and simply see a sea of sameness: hipster jeans, high heels, midriffs, big hoop earrings. By contrast, in Sri Lanka, everyone was eccentric and eclectic—when you met someone, you accepted a person in seersucker, shantung or sari. In Sri Lanka, people are conspicuously less obsessed with the material, it is not a culture of consumers. Making money isn't half as important as taking time out to praise the life you have.

The best part of visiting home, undoubtedly, was seeing my family. I spent days catching up on all their news, while I shared stories of my travels. Once reassured that they were all in good health, I left my hometown to throw myself again with gusto into the rest of my life. My thoughts turned gleefully to the elephant polo challenge ahead, being held once again at the height of Sri Lanka's winter. *Au fait* by now with Geoffrey's love of theatrics, I again enlisted the help of several Aussie friends, including loyal, trusty Anya who committed a second time for the week-long jumbo joust. This time we had my Sydney friends, Nic, Anna and Rowie, to cook and Janet as stylist, with Soos returning to help. My job was to oversee the lot.

Anya and I planned everything in such detail that I felt prepared for almost anything. We boarded our Colombo-bound flight weighed down with sufficient pots, pans, bain-maries, candles and shot glasses to guarantee a foolproof fiesta, a staggering 120 kilograms overweight on our baggage limit.

We were also looking forward to being reunited with familiar friends. Kristjan Edwards was flying in from Nepal; the Manclarks were representing Chivas Regal and there were a couple of new teams, including an Australian team and even an all-woman's team boasting a Thai princess. Tournament numbers were up and it was all systems go for a *pukka chukka* (first-class play)!

Two days before the event, my team and I prepared to drive south. This time, we had a refrigerated truck to help us cater for the polo festivities. No more minuscule fridges and overloaded eskies; Anya and I, who would be travelling separately, were positively gloating as we considered the degree of our foresightedness.

We were but 45 minutes into the journey, however, before my mobile phone rang. It was Anya, stuck on the side of the road, with a broken-down truck. I could hear the agitated honks and toots of traffic in the background as she described the steam pouring from the truck's engine, and I sighed. I asked my friend to keep me posted and the rest of us continued to speed southwards.

About an hour later, the phone rang again. It was Anya. 'When the truck's not going, the refrigerator's not going,' she said and I shuddered, imagining the thousands of dollars worth of sashimi, canapés, chocolates and chilled mousse spoiling in the heat.

Two hours later, Anya and truck were back on the road and we collectively sighed with relief, praying that our provisions were salvageable. That evening, discovering that all was well, we tucked into a huge feast of lobster on the beach and prepared for the next day's onslaught.

Geoffrey arrived in due course, with several team players in tow, and seemed horrified to discover I wasn't cooking every meal personally. I pointed out that someone needed to arrange the 101 other details that cropped up every minute of every single day and then, as if to prove my point, my mobile phone rang announcing yet another organisational hiccough.

The pesky refrigeration truck proved a constant headache; by day two of the polo tournament, it had become bogged on the beach between Weligama and Taprobane Island. It was no small task finding a tractor to pull it out of the sand before it became engulfed by rising tidal seawater.

I also fielded calls from the kitchen. 'Libby, I thought fillets of chicken came without bones? These ones have bones!' A bewildered Nic would state. I realised immediately that I should have warned my chefs of the local habits. 'And Libby ... the cream ... it's not whipping? It says whipping cream, but ...'

Poor Nic struggled to maintain calm as the team typically catered for 40, 50 or 60 hungry guests at one sitting. 'Libby, the gas bottle has run out. Where do we get some more gas? Libby, the cake in the oven—it's sunk.' My poor friend was boggled and my phone kept ringing. 'Libby, I thought we were getting capsicums? We've got enormous green chillies here, but there are no capsicums.'

I did my best, and the team rallied. For our first big party, we scattered pink bougainvillea leaves all over the floor, erected flares and Chinese lanterns, threw a long hot pink sash over a long white tablecloth and unwrapped the crockery. Huge, dirty tankards stinking like dead animals greeted the unpackers and Anya was sent bowling up the coast in search of something more appropriate for our guests. Geoffrey wanted a tournament to impress the most jaded jetsetter and he was going to get it!

When the Sri Lankan team won the international cup for the second year running, there was no one more delighted than the tournament host, Geoffrey Dobbs. It seemed appropriate to farewell the contestants with an enormous party on the shores of Taprobane Island, especially since they had flown all this way only to be trounced again.

Guests arrived for the grand finale dressed all in red as per the invitations, their crimson garb mirrored everywhere on the island. Every tree trunk was wrapped in red; there was red food, red drinks, a red carpet of flowers leading from the beach up the 103-step staircase, red drapes, tablecloths and red candles. Bagpipes squawked eerily in the twilight as kerosene wafted redolently in the breeze from the night flares.

When the last international guest departed, we collapsed triumphantly at another of Geoffrey's beautiful villas on the beach and lazily soaked up a week of unceasing sunshine. Yet again, the tournament had been a huge success, everyone had a lot of fun, my friends were filled with a sense of accomplishment and I was blissed out. Life was good—and it was great to be back.

Even better, Anya was also now part of my new life in Sri Lanka, having taken to the unpredictable rhythms of Colombo with open-minded enthusiasm. She was also working for Geoffrey, who would fly in and out of the country once or twice a month for a couple of days, leaving a trail of instructions in his wake. Anya was left to conceive, stock and revamp one of Geoffrey's cafes while I was charged with the launch of a sophisticated champagne and tapas bar in the heart of Colombo's tourist district.

And we got on with it. I registered a company name, scouted for locations, negotiated leases, met with architects and interior designers, wrote a business plan, devised menus, hunted for chefs, and learned more about bureaucracy than I ever care to learn again. With an impending election looming, no government department was approving anything—least of all architectural plans—and Geoffrey and I were left tearing our hair out with frustration.

Then, one of the restaurant chefs went psycho on Anya and I, informing us in no uncertain terms that he was not going to have women telling him what to do, and even worse, Western women on expat salaries. He was, he fumed, a brilliant chef earning far less than he was worth. 'I am not cooking no more Australian junk food,' our chef screamed as he brandished a kitchen knife alarmingly close to my nose.

That same week, not entirely coincidentally, two burly officers from the Department of Immigration visited Geoffrey's offices and demanded to see both Anya and I. This was a problem, as neither of us had switched over from tourist visas to work permits. Anya, by sheer luck, was up north with her sister on a sightseeing tour, while I was left to hand over my passport for inspection. It was promptly whisked away and I was told to report to the office of immigration the following morning.

I couldn't believe it! After all that work I was going to be deported? Collecting my wits and forcing myself to calm down, I called a close friend in the city and sure enough, he put me in touch with a good local lawyer.

I watched eagle-eyed the next day, my mouth zipped, as my new lawyer parried with the immigration officers in Sinhalese. I could barely understand a word of their conversation, but the body language told me things were looking good. Everyone would occasionally glance at me, the white-faced Western woman, as the comfortable ritual of tactical bargaining continued undeterred.

Finally, I was informed that due process would take place, but that essentially, US$500 would make the whole nasty business go away. I was also advised to fly to Australia for a while to lie low and this I did, but not before signing a 12-month lease for my first 'home' in Colombo. Undaunted by my brush with Sri Lanka's lawmakers, I planned to return as soon as possible.

By the time I returned to Colombo one month later—it was almost August by now—it was a relief. Australia had become easier to manage, in terms of the memories I had there, but it was still not a place to which I wished to return permanently. Not yet, anyway. Back home there was nowhere I could go, or anyone I could see, that didn't remind me of happy times gone terribly wrong. I would drive through suburbs where I had lived, worked, run, partied and lived life and I would feel the familiar pangs that had overwhelmed me after Justin, and then Paddy and Nato died. That old, awful feeling—that people connected to me were doomed—returned to haunt me.

By contrast, back in Colombo, I felt surrounded by bright colours, strong smells and vivid signs of life. I threw myself into work and a busy social life among a community of all cultural persuasions. There was Canadian-born Pat, talented photographer and interior designer who had lived in Sri Lanka for 20-odd years. When she heard about the elephant polo, she not only became the tournament's official photographer, she also joined the all-women's team.

There was larger-than-life Henri, manager of Geoffrey's hotels and villas. Hen, as we affectionately called her, loved nothing more than a party where she could don feathers, glitter and fairy wings or anything pink that took her fancy. She was madly in love with a handsome young Sri Lankan and together the pair embraced life with ardour. Hen enjoyed a life in Galle unrestrained by the conventions of her social circle back home. I understood exactly what she meant when she said, 'In Lanka, Lib, I feel free'.

There was 'Uncle' Gerry Delilkhan, a Sri Lankan-born journalist around 70 years of age who exuded enough energy to match at least three of me. Having covered most of Asia's key political events in his 45-year-long career, Uncle Gerry could converse knowledgeably about politics ad infinitum. Despite the fact that his favourite topic was cricket, he remained a close friend.

There was also Nimalka, a bright, chatty mother of two and recent divorcée with whom I worked. We would often swap stories at lunch over sushi, salad or the odd rice and curry. I would learn first-hand about husbands who 'lost face' if their wives worked; wives who lost social standing if they divorced their husbands; and how social taboos conspired to make it almost impossible for a Sri Lankan female to work and run a home.

All these insights notwithstanding, I was learning to love my erratic new regime of work and play and would look forward to the endless visitors on various missions, assignments or business forays who inevitably crossed my path as I began to mould a boutique travel business.

Anya and I were sharing a house and together we threw dinner parties that rocked until the wee hours, the scented night air filled with the laughter of guests as we recounted stories, travels, adventures and escapades. I cherished my new house and its enchanting garden filled with frangipani, squirrels and birds, but I also missed the fresh air and outdoor life of Australia.

I wasn't missing Sydney's cafes, brunches or nightlife; I wasn't missing the shopping, theatre or movies, but I was missing the open spaces in which I had so often walked, cycled or hiked. Colombo's humid weather, pollution, noisy population and general chaos did not lend itself to outdoor exercise and I found myself beginning to feel seriously unfit. I didn't like the feeling at all.

The day before my parents were due to arrive in Colombo for their first ever visit, Anya, Pat and I took ourselves to a nearby park to do some exercise. We had all decided we needed to do something drastic and had committed to getting together three times a week to egg each other on as we underwent a 50-minute exercise drill. I took on the role of chief lieutenant for our personal 'boot camp'.

Needless to say, at our first session, the three of us pushed ourselves beyond what was strictly necessary and went home exhausted but smug. When I woke the next morning feeling rotten and sore, I didn't think twice about it and looked forward instead to meeting my parents at the airport that night (midnight arrival, of course).

The following day, with my parents ensconced in their beautiful colonial boutique hotel, I awoke feeling worse and swallowed a couple of anti-inflammatories before taking my parents out sightseeing and then on to Colombo's finest restaurant for a welcome dinner. By now, I felt aches and pains all over; my back was killing me and it was becoming harder to remain cheerful. Convinced I had the flu, I decided to keep my discomfort to myself until my parents left the next day for hill country. I would collapse and recover then.

The following morning, relieved to know Mum and Dad were on their travels, I put myself to bed, admitting to Anya that I felt pretty damn rotten. When she returned from the office in the early evening, my body ached all over, my skin felt strangely metallic and I realised that something was seriously wrong. When Anya began to share my symptoms with friends, someone mentioned the word 'dengue'.

My body felt like lead, I couldn't even sit up properly on the way to hospital, but lay instead in Anya's lap. I was whisked into emergency where they took a blood sample, and then just as quickly told to go home and rest and call later for the results. I did as I was told but the results didn't look good, and before I knew it I was back at the hospital. Barely able to move by then, I was relieved to be placed in a wheelchair and admitted as a patient.

Finally, the blood tests confirmed that a dengue-carrying mosquito had done its dastardly work and from then on, it was as if everyone from the Chief Superintendent down was intent on restoring me to my former good health. Weak and sick as I was, it didn't escape me how fortunate I was to be admitted to Apollo Hospital, one of a well-regarded Asian hospital chain that deserved the hotel equivalent of five-star.

As the hours passed, my condition detriorated. My teeth felt like they were being ripped from my gums. The tip of my nose felt like it was about to snap off. My eyeballs were sore. The tips of my fingers hurt. Every joint in my body ached and I couldn't hide it any more. I was in agony. Plus, I couldn't stop vomiting. Just when I thought I had absolutely nothing left to bring up, I would vomit again. Exhausted and in great pain, I endured blood tests every two hours, submitted to ultrasounds and X-rays, watched the drip steadily feed its sugar-laden liquid into me and saw my arms get blacker and bluer as needle after needle plunged into my skin.

Anya, eyes like saucers and with an attitude that would have done Florence Nightingale proud, tried to keep the bad news away from my parents as long as possible. However, as my platelet count began to plummet and I drifted in and out of consciousness, one of the doctors insisted my parents were called.

By day eight, my platelet count was perilously close to zero, and the specialists suggested a blood transfusion. At first I baulked at this suggestion, yielding to all the stereotypical fears about third world countries, especially those pertaining to disease and contamination.

As I was not getting better, however, it became obvious that I did not have much choice. To get over my dengue I might pick up the HIV virus, but that was a risk I was going to have to take.

By now, my worried parents were at the bedside of their pale, bruised, stick-thin daughter. I felt overcome with love and emotion for them. Mum and Dad had nursed me through so many personal disasters, I was almost relieved that this was only dengue fever. I might have felt as brittle as glass, but I felt in my heart of hearts that I was going to pull through.

After a third blood transfusion my private prediction started to actualise as my blood platelet count began, ever so slowly, to rise. My appetite returned and the vomiting abated, my parents were despatched to continue their holiday and Anya finally let off steam after days and nights at my bedside.

The doctor strongly recommended that I leave Sri Lanka never to return because, he said, I might not survive another bout of dengue. Alternatively, he commanded me to wear long-sleeved clothing at all times and to install mosquito screens on all my home's doors and windows. I was also instructed to sleep under a mosquito net for the rest of my Sri Lankan life. Given that dengue is often fatal I knew I was lucky. Still, Anya and I could only laugh ruefully. Honestly, there seemed no end to what we had endured together.

Six weeks later, as Christmas approached, Anya and I decided to celebrate the occasion in our new homeland, Geoffrey invited us to spend Christmas Day on Taprobane Island with him and his family. With arrangements already made for the morning, we were thrilled to be able to make Christmas dinner. We also liked the idea of a holiday event that we would not have to host ourselves; for once, we would be the guests.

Since Justin's death, I tended to dread Christmas. The day always reminded me of the desolation I had felt my first Christmas without him, despite being surrounded by family and friends. This festive season however, I was a free agent, flitting from social occasion to social occasion, swapping champagne flute for wine glass, and tucking into strawberries, turkey, ham, dhal, chicken curry and coconut sambal, depending on where I was.

Christmas on Taprobane would be a glorious break from my usual Christmas tradition back home with family, with the promise of more delicious food and drink among friends on an island at sunset. On Christmas night, I collapsed into bed after a glorious, fun day, with high hopes for the year ahead.

The morning of 26 December 2004 dawned and everyone went walking or swimming before breakfast to work off the previous day's fare. Geoffrey had gone for a run and his mother, Marie, brother Michael, sister-in-law Lisa, Anya and I went for a walk along the beach before breakfast.

As we strolled along in various small groups, we all noticed an extraordinary number of bats and crows nestled in the trees as well as many birds wheeling furiously in the sky. It was unusual and we wondered what their presence signified. We didn't think about it for long however, as the day was glorious, the sky a picturebook blue and the ocean turquoise and calm.

Returning from our walk at around 9 am, Geoffrey, Michael and Lisa decided to go for a swim in the sea while the rest of us headed back to the island for a dip in the swimming pool. As I dived in and surfaced refreshed from the water, I noticed a large rip in the sea surrounding us. With no time to bring it to anyone's attention, I then saw the rip turn into a big, brown swell that advanced upon us swiftly and ominously. Within seconds, the swell reached our island and swept across it, lifting all of us swimmers at least a metre or more out of the swimming pool. By sheer good fortune, all of us were thrown onto higher ground.

I was able to find my footing and immediately ran towards the villa perched on the island's highest point. I looked around and saw everyone else running along beside me. Once we had established that we were safe, we looked around and saw the same brown swell hitting the mainland.

What followed next I will never forget for the rest of my life. I could hear people screaming, dogs yelping, the sound of timber cracking, dull thuds and roars as dwellings crumbled under the onslaught of water. It was all happening very fast and before any of us could say a word or spring to action, we watched the swell reverse. Within seconds, the entire Bay of Weligama was drained and we were all staring in complete bewilderment at the bottom of the ocean floor.

I looked around in the confusion to check that everyone was accounted for and remembered then, with a sickening thud in my stomach, that Geoffrey, Michael and Lisa had gone swimming. Where were they?

Cries of anguish continued to reach us faintly from the mainland and we gazed in mute shock at the devastation that one freak wave had caused in so short a time.

Intuitively I knew that this had been something extraordinary, but it was only many hours later, when my mother called me on my mobile phone that I first heard the word 'tsunami'. By then, I could report that everyone in my group was, miraculously, alive and well.

Geoffrey, his brother and sister-in-law had survived despite their morning ocean swim. When the killer wave hit, the brothers had clung to a fishing catamaran that had lodged itself between a palm tree and the roof of a house. Geoffrey's sister-in-law, slightly separate from the pair, had also clung for dear life to a palm tree and escaped with only superficial leg wounds. Ears still ringing from the wails and shrieks that had filled the air during the sudden onslaught, the shaken trio had managed to climb aboard Taprobane's completely mangled jetty.

None of us was able to immediately process the events of that extraordinary day. We were all relatively unscathed and, yes, the sun was still shining brightly outside in a perfectly blue sky, but it was clear that everything was now irrevocably different.

CHAPTER THIRTEEN
NO TIME TO REST

On the night of 26 December 2004, as in most parts of Southeast Asia, a mournful mood descended on the residents of Taprobane. Ocean waves continued to crash ominously on the rocks of our tiny promontory and we all found it difficult to settle down and sleep. Every crash on the mainland made our hearts jump ... was that normal surf or another killer wave? We had no means of getting off the island except by foot, yet all of us wanted nothing more than to get as far away as possible from the water's edge. I was receiving SMS messages begging me to get off the island, but I was determined to stay calm. For now, we had a hot, muggy and mosquito-laden night to endure.

As night fell, I became aware I had a stomachache. I put it down to stress and trauma, retiring to bed early to try and sleep it off, but as the hours passed, the pain in my stomach increased to a point where I could no longer ignore it. I was sitting up in bed, then standing, rolling over and lying on my side ... nothing made me feel better. I didn't know what was wrong with me, but having suffered similar pain with an ovarian cyst in the past, I put it down to another possible flare-up. This possibility served only to mildly allay my concerns, however, as I knew I would need serious medical attention if the pain continued to worsen.

At about 5 am, a restless Geoffrey awoke, took one look at me and realised that something needed to be done. He and Anya immediately set off on foot to get help. While I waited, I sat or lay silently, willing myself to say little to those around me about the pain I was in. When reports were constantly coming in about the devastation that had been wrought on the mainland, and we could still hear the wails of suffering in the distance, it seemed utterly inane to be complaining. Meanwhile, Geoffrey's relatives had started packing in preparation to leave Taprobane. After what had happened, Geoffrey's Washington-based brother, wife and children were hardly in the mood for a holiday. As everyone milled around listlessly, unable to eat or muster any gaiety, Geoffrey's niece, Olivia, picked up a guitar and started singing a melancholic song. As we sat and listened, tears began to slowly course down my face. And then I noticed that everyone else was crying too.

Up until then, none of us had cried, too numb with shock to take in what was happening all around us. We had been the lucky ones who had survived while thousands were in desperate need. What to do? We were indeed leaving Weligama, a shaken and sorry lot, and Olivia's song finally allowed us all to express our sadness.

By the time Anya and Geoffrey returned, all of us were packed and ready to go. Geoffrey had been able to arrange transport, even at such a chaotic time, for me to leave the island, in a van that was already transporting five mildly injured passengers back to Colombo. I climbed in the front of the van and as we departed I took in, for the first time, the extent of the havoc the Boxing Day tsunami had wrought. Despite my painkiller-induced grogginess, I couldn't avoid seeing sights that made my wrenching stomach pains pale in comparison. Dead bodies, wreathed in flies, lay everywhere along the side of the road; hopeless-looking people stared at the convoy of vehicles that drove by, while others stood in queues outside temples in search of solace, a patch of shade, a roof over their heads or somewhere to contemplate their fate in peace.

Some bodies were already being buried in quick, makeshift ceremonies. We could also see people carrying goods from destroyed shops and buses up ended by the tsunami with passengers, cut and bleeding, still lying dazed under nearby trees. Shattered fish markets lay strewn in chaos, broken boats were piled in heaps all along the coast and the stench of rotting bodies, when we dared to open a window, was pervasive. In my exhausted, drugged state, all of it whirled around me like a bad dream. I wanted to wake up and find it wasn't real—that everything was as tranquil as it had been on Christmas Day—but alas, the nightmare was authentic.

As the roads became impassable we turned inland and discovered, to our amazement, scenes in complete contrast to the devastation on the coast. Farmers tended to their paddy fields, shops were full of produce and life continued as on any normal day. Our van chugged through the lush terraced hill country and despite my pain, I felt awe-struck by the beauty I saw all around me. This island realm had just endured one of recent history's worst natural disasters, but this fact did not detract from the breathtaking scenery we traversed that day. Perhaps because of the contrast to the horror we had witnessed just a few kilometres before, I will always remember our journey through the hinterland as one of the most moving, scenic drives I've ever experienced.

The journey from Weligama to Colombo usually took around four hours, but after five hours we were only halfway there and I was desperately trying to stay alert and in control. Our driver stopped so that we could all stretch our legs and as I unfurled in agony from the front seat a stranger asked if I required medical attention. I explained my symptoms and the man called a doctor over. Within seconds, I was prone on the floor of a cafeteria surrounded by curious strangers as a doctor peppered me with questions. I nearly threw up with pain at one point when he prodded me, but managed by sheer will to keep my extreme discomfort to myself. Once finished, the doctor gave me a script for antibiotics: I had appendicitis. Great, I thought. Great timing.

Finally, almost 24 hours after my first twinges of pain, I was wheeled into the local hospital. Despite this being where a friend of a friend, Dr Jerry Jayasekara, operated, I was frightened by what I perceived as unhygienic hospital conditions. When I voiced my concerns to Dr Jerry, he was brisk and unsympathetic.

'Look dear, the choice is yours. This is who I am and you need to make your decision quickly, as I'm about to go home. I will return in ten minutes and you need to let me know. Your condition is serious, your appendix has burst, so let's not waste time.'

I looked around me and could sense a frenzy building as injured people began to slowly filter into the foyer, waiting rooms and corridors of this run-down hospital. I looked up at the ceiling, gazed at the peeling paint and stared at patients attached to antiquated equipment, being wheeled by. All I wanted, I realised, was Dr Jerry to operate on me and make the pain go away. As I lay in bed waiting to be wheeled into surgery, my mobile phone continued to ring. I was keeping my calls brief, steeling myself with every ring to hear that someone I knew had not made it. After all, my friends were strung all along the coastline. When news came through that yet another had survived the disaster I felt moved to cry.

Like a child, I asked Dr Jerry if I would be okay and he took my hand in his and reassured me. 'Of course you will be okay, I will look after you like you are my very own daughter'. Consoled by these words, I finally, thankfully, lost consciousness.

Hours later I awoke in a dingy, grotty ward, in pain, and surrendered myself to the process of convalescence. After four days, filled with visits from friends who provided much-needed relief, another friend from the Australian High Commission called to inform me that a plane had been arranged to fly back to Australia that night—did I wish to climb aboard? After discussing it with my trio of hard-core best buddies—Anya, Kath and Sammy (the same Sammy who had been with me all those years ago when Justin first declared his love, now on holiday in Sri Lanka)—I let myself be persuaded that I would be better off in Australia.

Awful stories were circulating about the thousands dead and the possible spread of disease. It wasn't unusual for a friend to call from a nearby supermarket to describe the mad panic in the aisles as locals stacked up on emergency provisions in preparation for the possibility of another tsunami. My girlfriends were desperate to leave Serendip's shores and the more I heard, the more convinced I was that I would be better off recuperating somewhere safer.

Lying helplessly in my hospital bed as the hours ticked by until our flight, I followed news reports that came in via television and radio of the horrors of the tsunami. I saw the graphic visuals being broadcast of the human and physical wreckage left behind by the killer wave— the overriding message coming through, as it appeared to me then, was that there was little practical help on the ground for the thousands of tsunami survivors. Like many others, I was appalled by both the scope of the disaster and the apparent lack of readiness by the authorities to deal with it.

Finally, just after 7 pm, Kath, Sammy, Anya and I were hurtling along a main city route to the airport. I was hobbling on the tarmac when my phone rang for the billionth time. This time it was Geoffrey. 'This is my idea Libby. Adopt Sri Lanka. What do you think?'

I stopped dead in my tracks. What on earth was Geoffrey talking about?

'Adopt Sri Lanka. You know! Adopt a home, adopt a school, adopt a boat, and help the people however you can. Make a difference, fish and ships!'

Geoffrey was leaving a lot unsaid, but I got it all the same. 'Terrific idea, Geoffrey,' I began.

'I want a website, www.adoptsrilanka.com as soon as possible. Tell the press and tell the world. Start developing it all. I will email you.' And he was gone. My mind was whirling. I felt an enormous surge of guilt that I was running away from Sri Lanka at a time of crisis, but I also knew deep down that I was too sick to be of much use to anyone here. Maybe … just maybe … Geoffrey's idea was the way to go?

Back in Australia I was enormously relieved to find myself safe and secure in my parents' Camden idyll. But as the extent of the tsunami was relayed on our television screen day and night, I also became emotional and upset. Very quickly, I realised that I couldn't comfortably watch the footage of the tsunami aftermath. There were too many deaths, too much destruction, too much suffering, and I had seen too much of it first-hand. Once again I found myself asking the sort of questions that can never be satisfyingly explained. How could this happen? Why did so many innocent people have to suffer? What was happening to Mother Nature?

Since Justin's death, I had lost confidence in my personal world. Now I was losing confidence in the physical world around me. But even as these pointless, negative thoughts were whirling around in my head, I could hear that familiar internal voice urging me to do something positive.

So I did, much to the distress of my parents who simply wanted their youngest to convalesce in peace. I set up a website for Geoffrey within days and then got on the phone to journalists all over the world. Daily, I answered hundreds of emails from correspondents who wanted to help. Geoffrey's network of contacts was invaluable and the media were also keen to show their support for the thousands of families left destitute on the shores of Serendip.

It didn't take long before hundreds, then thousands, then hundreds of thousands of dollars, began to pour in to support Geoffrey's grassroots vision to help the suffering in Sri Lanka. As the initial trickle very quickly became a groundswell, I became energised and inspired by all the goodwill pouring in for AdoptSriLanka. My dengue frailty was forgotten, my post-appendicitis stitches ignored and eight hours' sleep at night became something rarer than a tree in the Gobi desert! And at the centre of it all, as usual, was my frenetic, crazy, indefatigable and completely wonderful employer and friend, Geoffrey Dobbs. During those initial weeks Geoffrey contacted every single influential person he knew. Thanks largely to his efforts, in conjunction with other local businessmen, AdoptSriLanka was able to provide humanitarian aid within a fortnight of the disaster to over 8500 people living in temporary camps.

Aid was typically in the form of food, shelter or money for repairs—above all, we concentrated on helping people to regain their means of livelihood by fishing, sewing or growing and selling produce. If people needed a sewing machine fixed; a school uniform for a child; a roof repaired; a new boat; or help with their market produce stall, somehow AdoptSriLanka would find a way.

Before we could catch our breath, Geoffrey then launched another initiative: the AdoptSriLanka Twins Project, a philanthropic scheme that concentrated on schools abroad helping to rebuild devastated 'twin' sister schools locally. Thanks to donations, volunteers and a network of 'can do' friends and supporters, money was channelled swiftly to do good where it was needed most. School buildings were repaired; desks and chairs fixed; thousands of schoolbooks delivered to dozens of schools; and a little sewing 'army' of women provided with fabric and sewing machines so that the villages could prepare for another school term and return to semi-normal life.

During this time, Geoffrey was flying between the United Kingdom and Sri Lanka a couple of times a month while I was coordinating the website and responding to email correspondence from all over the world. I was also helping to channel the financial donations via various charity organisations that were set up speedily in the aftermath of the disaster in the United Kingdom, Spain, the United States and Australia.

Midway through January, Geoffrey continued his philanthropic mission with typical panache when he held a spectacularly successful publicity stunt at the House of Commons in London. At the opening of a Parliamentary sitting one dark, dank day, members of the lower house were regaled at lunch with a delicious Sri Lankan fish curry produced with the help of Sri Lanka's Ministry for Fisheries in conjunction with key corporate companies and Britain's largest fishing co-ops. The message of Operation Fish and Ships was simple: support Lanka's fish industry and help people rebuild their lives.

In addition to this, back in Sri Lanka, a delegation of fishermen was arranged to meet the Sri Lankan President and Cabinet, as well as the leader of the opposition, and hosted a sushi sunset dinner party for the diplomatic community. Simultaneously, a barbecue was held with fishermen in the south, which was successful in raising two pressing issues: the plight of the fishermen and their livelihood, and the need to quash any rumours that fish from the sea were unsafe to eat.

The publicity stunt got a lot of media coverage and the exposure intensified when ITN London ran a documentary two weeks later on Geoffrey and his vision of ordinary people, helped by philanthropic donations, doing humanitarian work on the ground. The response to the television broadcast was overwhelming: hundreds of people contacted our website offering money, time, provisions, clothing, services. The documentary was so moving that ITN broadcast it twice again in the next two months and each time the response was phenomenal. From very big corporates to pensioners in council houses—everyone, it seemed, wanted to help.

And as usual, I was running around like crazy, trying to make as much happen from afar without losing energy, perspective or my sense of humour. My parents weren't laughing as they watched their daughter hobble around from pillar to post, and my friends and relatives weren't amused that I was never available for social occasions, but there was simply too much to do.

The work paid off because within three months of the tsunami, our tiny humanitarian organisation had channelled close to US$3 million into various schemes including housing projects (135 new homes built, 140 renovated and rebuilt); fishing projects (116 new boats purchased, 87 repaired, 65 new nets, 3 boat yards established); and had provided funds to build, rebuild or expand hospital, school and orphanage facilities.

Thanks to AdoptSriLanka donations over 1200 individuals were helped and a trauma outreach clinic was established. Temples and churches were repaired and coastal conservation projects were also launched—in all, we planted 100,000 mangroves and 200,000 pandanus plants in order to restore turtle habitats in Rekawa and Kosgoda. Geoffrey and I also had the challenge of coordinating and employing more than 150 volunteers in the island's southern region.

Late one night, six weeks before I was due to return to Sri Lanka, reeling after a long day that rendered me sleepless—the scenes of those faces I had seen from our van on 27 December playing over and over again in my mind—I called Sammy to discuss an idea that had begun to percolate.

'I want to do something else to help. I'm thinking a fund-raising bash, here in Sydney…'

I jumped on the phone to a few more friends the following day and we brainstormed ideas. Finally, we determined that we would only hold a fundraising event if everything—and we meant everything—was donated free of charge. I'd heard about too many fundraisers where a small fortune was raised on the night, but pitifully little trickled, after costs, to the beneficiaries.

We decided as a group that we would get an MC, venue, food, alcohol, entertainment, a band, great donations for auction, the whole kit and caboodle for nothing, and we'd maximise our input to stricken families back in Lanka. After all, this was AdoptSriLanka's greatest selling point: that it quickly channelled money to the people who needed it most.

When I announced to my parents that I was now stage-directing a fundraiser to be held on the eve of my return voyage to Sri Lanka, I thought my mother was going to faint. It was hard to convince her that I felt compelled, after seeing the commitment of so many others, to do all I could. I had survived the tsunami and countless thousands hadn't; in fact, I hadn't lost a single possession and still had a house and family. And, well blow me down, I was happy with my life! Amid the rush of organisation and deadlines it hadn't occurred to me until now, but it was true. I really was happy.

By the time I stood up on the night of 12 March 2005 in front of a crowd of 350, I was exultant. We had pulled it off! Every guest at our prestige venue, colourfully decorated in flowers, was treated to food prepared by one of Australia's top caterers; the band was jumping, and the fabulous auction lots drew a great response from the crowd. One of the guests walked off, very happy, with tickets for a luxurious Sri Lankan holiday in boutique hotels and villas; another with a dinner party for six hosted by the editor of *Vogue Entertaining and Travel*, and another with a sailing holiday around the Whitsunday Islands for himself and five friends.

I got up to thank everyone for an amazing party and managed, for once, to hold back the tears. Everyone had always told me that I was remarkably calm and dignified at Justin's funeral; I was determined to be dignified now, too. As I looked around at the faces of the friends who had helped me to pull off this vibrant event, I felt overwhelmed by a strange mixture of happiness, sadness and pride. Afterwards, I was delighted to take with me back to Sri Lanka, a cheque for just over $120,000, contributing to the total US$3 million AdoptSriLanka had raised in the three months since the tsunami.

By the time I returned to Colombo towards the end of March 2005, the scope of the devastation was becoming clear. In total, the killer wave took 300,000 lives. In Sri Lanka alone, within 5 minutes, more than 30,000 people were killed, one million became homeless, 1200 children lost both their parents, while 100,000 houses and 165 schools were destroyed. In addition, over 50 per cent of the registered Sri Lankan fishing fleet was wiped out. At the time the tsunami struck the country had an already high unemployment level of approximately 60 per cent. With the tsunami's impact on the country's two key industries, fishing and tourism, this statistic soared.

I spent my time travelling up and down the island's devastated peninsula, gingerly driving around a coastline that now made me feel decidedly nervous. I was also apprehensive about swimming in the ocean, my heart stopping if a big wave approached, but I knew it was my mind playing games. Better, I thought, to concentrate on making sure AdoptSriLanka's projects went full steam ahead.

As I plunged onward, I came face to face with the good, the bad and the ugly aspects of aid work. I'd heard about the jealousies, petty bureaucracy and general negativity that typically reared their heads when different so-called humanitarian groups competed to provide help in times of disaster, but I was dismayed to experience for myself the degree to which people tended to focus on problems rather than solutions. Geoffrey and I would often look at each other and shake our heads in frustration and despair.

Fortunately, our initiative was of a size that we were able to avoid much of the interference that plagues other non-government organisations; whenever possible, the pair of us just kept our heads down and got on with it. We lived for the times when we could tell locals that we were able to help with a boat, a home, some money, clothes, food or education.

I particularly liked the Swim Lanka project that focused on teaching children how to swim. The brainchild of Julian Bolling, a former Olympic swimming champion, AdoptSriLanka was helping to build public swimming pools in the south of Sri Lanka, mainly around Weligama, Tangalle and Galle so that locals could be taught swimming and life-saving and generally overcome their fear of water.

I thought my heart was going to burst when the first swimming pool funded by AdoptSriLanka was opened. As I gazed at the photographs of children splashing about in the water, I couldn't think of a better way to help these young people get over their horrific experience. We may have been bruised and battered from the politics of humanitarian work, but Geoffrey and I could see for ourselves that we were making a difference.

In the midst of all this activity, probably because I was radiating a new sense of purpose and pleasure, I began a new romance with an extroverted, gregarious guy from Australia. It was my first relationship since losing Justin. My new boyfriend could not have had an easy time of it, with my tacit comparisons to my handsome, athletic and emotionally intelligent former boyfriend; however, I felt we were right for each other at that time in our lives. Although the romance was short-lived we parted amicably, with me feeling infinitely better prepared for a more significant relationship. My heart was open again.

I would never have chosen the path my life has followed. The deaths of close friends are hard enough to get over, but after I lost Justin I thought I had lost my future too. There's no doubt his death changed the course of my life. If he had lived, I would be a different person today.

But what I came, finally, to understand, is that the life I have now, the person I have become, is something to be valued. It's not second best. It's not just a way of keeping busy in place of my real life, the future I once held dear. This is it. And I like it.

I'm no saint. I still get as crazed and frantic as I ever did, and I still feel sad for what's been lost. But I also feel joy and love and peace.

As hard as the journey was, it has brought me a profound understanding of myself and what I have to contribute to the world. I wish Justin and Paddy and Nato, and all the others taken too soon, could sit with me in my lush tropical garden, sipping tea and watching the squirrels race around. But I know that what they would have wanted for me—indeed, demanded of me—was to be happy; to be able to open myself to life again. And I know that if they could see me now, they would rejoice.

ADOPT SRI LANKA –
HOW YOU CAN HELP

If you've bought this book you've already helped the work of AdoptSriLanka, which Libby was instrumental in setting up, since some of the proceeds go to furthering its work. Thank you.

The organisation was set up in response to the devastation caused by the tsunami of 26 December 2004, which took the lives of more than 30,000 people in Sri Lanka alone, destroyed one million homes and 165 school buildings, and wrecked more than half of the fishing fleet on which the country is so dependent.

AdoptSriLanka is made up of locals and expatriates working in and with local communities. Having successfully helped tens of thousands of people in the immediate aftermath of the tsunami, the organisation's focus is now on mid- to long-term projects that encourage and support self-sufficiency. Some of the key initiatives are:

■ **Twins School Program** has so far matched up 82 Sri Lankan schools with 'twin' schools overseas. As well as repairing buildings and equipment, the project directs help to individual students in need of books, uniforms and other education essentials.

■ **Project Fish and Ships** works on rebuilding the devastated fishing industry by providing materials, expertise and new boats. Among many things, a boat yard in Galle has been set up where large trawlers are being purpose-built. To date, six trawlers have been built in this boat yard and launched.

■ **Swim Lanka** is a recent innovation and is dear to Libby's heart. It teaches people to swim and to overcome their fear of water. The need is great in this traumatised island where many locals cannot swim. So far the project has placed four new fibreglass pools in the Trincomalee and Tangalle areas and more than 1000 children have enrolled for lessons. The next stage of the plan is to build and staff three 8-lane, 25-metre public swimming pools on the south coast.

More than 95 per cent of funds donated to AdoptSriLanka reach those in need. Contributions made through the specified channels are tax-deductible for Australian, UK, US and Spanish residents. For more information, and to donate, visit www.adoptsrilanka.com.

ACKNOWLEDGMENTS

This book would not have happened if it weren't for our mutual friend David Sweeney, who introduced us. Nor would the idea have progressed if wise and wonderful Melisande Clarke had not provided encouragement every step of the way, or if Murdoch Books's commissioning editor Hazel Flynn had not 'got it'. After that, it was pretty plain sailing as we embarked on a great adventure together, ably abetted and supported by great people like Anya Rowlands, Prabal Thapa, Geoffrey Dobbs, MaryAnn Ellis, Jan McDonald, Prue Crookes, Kath Englert, Sammy Jones, Georgie O'Shea, Granny, Andrew Peacock and legal eagle John Bleechmore. What good sports all of you are ... thank you. Josephine's husband, Steve Allen, was also invaluable throughout the nine-month gestation, proving to be a rock of support, as usual. And finally it was the team at Murdoch—Jacqueline Blanchard, Lauren Camilleri, Kay Scarlett and Juliet Rogers—who made it come alive. Our heartfelt thanks to all of you for your integrity and understanding.

— Libby and Josephine

Libby Southwell

Libby Southwell is currently working in Sri Lanka running businesses in up-market tourism.

Josephine Brouard

Josephine Brouard is a Sydney-based freelance writer and editor. Visit www.josephinebrouard.com.

First published in 2006 by Pier 9
an imprint of Murdoch Books Pty Limited

Murdoch Books Pty Limited Australia
Pier 8/9, 23 Hickson Road, Millers Point NSW 2000
Phone: +61 (0) 2 8220 2000 Fax: +61 (0) 2 8220 2558

Chief Executive: Juliet Rogers
Publishing Director: Kay Scarlett

Commissioning Editor: Hazel Flynn
Design Manager: Vivien Valk
Concept and Design: Lauren Camilleri
Editor: Jacqueline Blanchard
Production: Monika Paratore

National Library of Australia Cataloguing-in-Publication Data
Southwell, Libby.— Monsoon rains and icicle drops
ISBN 1 74045 789 7. ISBN 9 78174045 7897.
1. Southwell, Libby - Travel. 2. Self-perception.
3. Self-actualization (Psychology). I. Brouard, Josephine. II. Title. 158.1

Printed by Midas Printing (Asia) Ltd. PRINTED IN CHINA.
First printed 2006. Reprinted 2006 (twice).

Page 119: *Lonely Planet Sri Lanka*, Lonely Planet Publications,
Melbourne, 2002.
Page 148: Gregson, J 2003, *Blood Against the Snows: The Tragic
Story of Nepal's Royal Dynasty*, Fourth Estate, page xi.
Pages 158–160: Dunham, C & Baker, I (Photography Kelly, T) 2001,
Tibet: Reflections from the Wheel of Life, Abbeville Press, New York.
Page 165: *Lonely Planet Tibet* (5th edn), Lonely Planet Publications,
2002.
Page 202: *Lonely Planet Mongolia* (3rd edn), Lonely Planet
Publications, 2001.

Photographs: Jason Lowe (front cover), Georgia O'Shea (page 5),
Richard Powers (page 279 left), Andrew Lehmann/Notebook
(page 279 right), Alan Benson (back cover).